Friends & Lovers Cookbook

Nancy Fair McIntyre

Illustrations by William Alexander

GALA BOOKS
2147 Laguna Canyon Road
Laguna Beach, California 92652

All rights reserved. Illustrations and text,
or any portions thereof, may not be reproduced
in any form without permission of the publisher.

Library of Congress Catalog Number: 76-17412
ISBN Number: 0-912448-08-3
Copyright 1976 Gala Books
Composed and Printed in the United States of America

Table of Contents

Introduction	5
Chapter I	
Budget Cooking for Married Lovers	6
Chapter II	
Living Together on Love and Vegetables	22
Chapter III	
Slow Cookery and Fast Meals for the Working Couple	39
Chapter IV	
The Singles Scene	55
Chapter V	
The Gourmet Dude	77
Chapter VI	
City Lunches and Country Picnics	94
Index	114

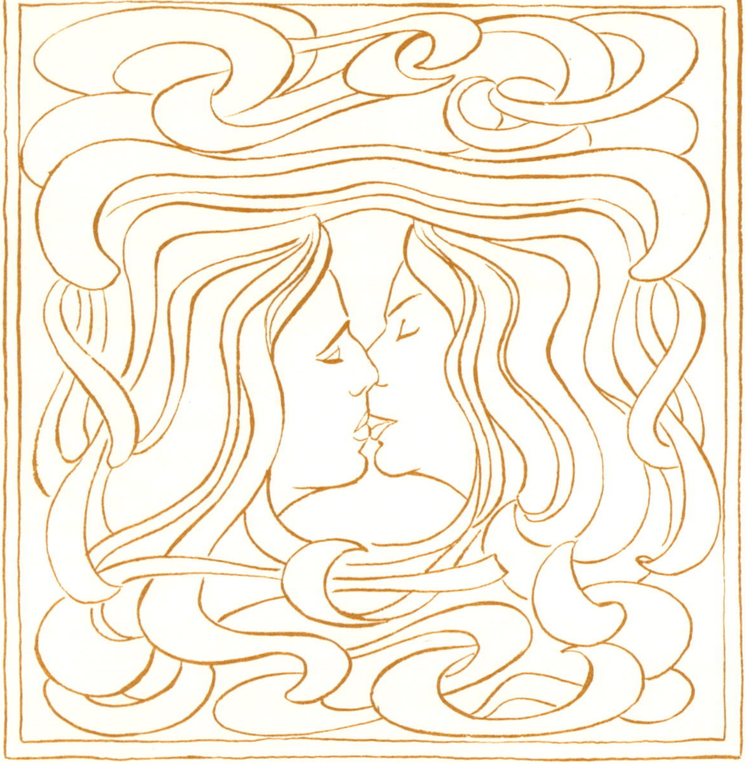

Introduction

To Each His Own

This is a lifestyle cookbook for married lovers, unmarried lovers, just good friends, working couples, liberated singles, gourmet bachelors, platonic roommates and loving vegetarians. Keyed to today's living, Friends & Lovers embraces every variety of cooking: fast, slow, extravagant and broke.

There are considerate dishes for the newlywed budget and crock pot dinners for working couples. There are vegetarian delights for herbivores and gourmet spectaculars for predatory bachelors. And for the liberated single woman, we offer tasty banquets for one, as well as starcrossed dinners for two. *Friends & Lovers* also wraps up some new ideas for brown bag lunches and country picnics to help you escape the restaurant crunch.

Though we open a few cans along the way, this is basically a book of good nutrition where fresh is best. All recipes easily adapt to organic ingredients. While primarily for couples or singles, most portions are based on four servings since it is cheaper and more convenient to cook for several meals and refrigerate or freeze the leftovers—especially with soups and casseroles.

Be you friend or lover—or happily both—here's special fare to fit your lifestyle and budget.

Chapter 1

Budget Cooking for Married Lovers

Some lovers defy convention and get married. If life in the rose-covered cottage is short on cash, it's long on ingenuity. Eating well on a lean budget is a triumph of imagination over hot dog, burger and packaged dinner. Happily, many of the great dishes of the world are pennysaving feasts. Consider the great homemade soups, the rich pastas, and the meat-stretching casseroles and stir-frys. If wedded bliss can conquer mother-in-laws and mortgages, it can certainly conquer a mean budget.

Monday Night Meatball

*When your legal lover can't face another hamburger,
vary the daily grind with this unique meatball-and-vegetable soup.*

**1/2 lb ground round
1 tsp parsley, chopped
1/4 tsp thyme
1/2 tsp salt
1/2 tsp pepper
1 egg yolk, beaten
2 Tbsp margarine
2 small carrots, peeled
1 rib of celery
2 green onions
1 small beet, peeled
2 small potatoes, peeled
1/2 cup fresh green beans
6 cups beef broth
Garnish: chopped parsley**

Mix ground round with parsley, thyme, salt, pepper and egg yolk. Shape meat into 1-inch meatballs. Melt margarine in skillet and quickly brown meatballs. Cut carrots, celery, onions, beet and potatoes into 1 1/2 inch long, thin strips, Julienne style. Cut green beans into 1-inch lengths. Bring broth to a simmer and add vegetables. Simmer 15 minutes. Add meatballs and simmer another 10 minutes. Garnish with parsley. Makes 4 servings.

Baked Eggs Florentine

A work of art from Florence that is price-less.

10-oz package frozen chopped spinach
1 Tbsp margarine
2 Tbsp green onions, finely chopped
2 Tbsp margarine
2 Tbsp flour

1 cup milk
1/4 cup Parmesan cheese, grated
1/2 tsp salt
4 eggs
2 Tbsp Parmesan cheese, grated

Cook spinach according to package directions. Press out all excess moisture with a slotted spoon. Melt margarine in a skillet, and saute onions until tender. Combine onions, margarine and spinach. Divide spinach equally in two buttered, individual baking dishes. Melt margarine in saucepan and stir in flour. Gradually add milk and stir until sauce thickens. Sprinkle in cheese, season with salt, and stir until sauce is smooth. Spoon sauce equally over eggs and top with remaining Parmesan cheese. Bake eggs in a preheated 350 degree oven for 10 minutes or until eggs are fairly firm on the outside but still soft inside. Serves 2.

Homemade Fettucine with Mushroom Sauce

Italian men claim there are two things that keep a woman happy,
a good man and a good pasta.

3 cups all-purpose flour
3 eggs, slightly beaten
3 qts water
1 Tbsp salt
1 Tbsp olive oil

Sift flour. Make a mound of flour on a pastry board, with a depression in the middle. Pour eggs into the depression. Knead dough with your hands until it is satiny and smooth, about 10 minutes. Divide dough in half and form into 2 balls. Wrap in wax paper and let stand at room temperature 1 hour. Roll out each ball of dough, on a lightly floured board, into a rectangle about 14 x 16 inches. Roll up the rectangle tightly, like a jelly roll, starting with the 14 inch side. Cut into strips 1/2 inch wide. Gently separate strips of dough and allow to dry for a couple of hours. Bring 3 qts water to a gentle boil and pour in salt and olive oil. Drop handfuls of noodles into water and cook 4 or

5 minutes until just tender. (A 16th century gourmet advised that pasta be cooked just long enough to say a short prayer.) Do not overcook or the noodles will turn mushy. Drain fettucine and spoon over the following fresh Mushroom Sauce which should be hot and ready before you cook the fettucine. Sprinkle fettucine with a liberal topping of Parmesan cheese before serving.

Mushroom Sauce

1 cup white onions, thinly sliced
1/3 cup butter, melted
3 cups fresh mushrooms, thinly sliced
1 1/2 cups heavy cream
Salt & pepper to taste

Saute onions in butter until golden. Add mushrooms and cook until tender. Pour in heavy cream and bring to a simmer. Season with salt & pepper to taste. Pasta and sauce serves 4.

Pasta & Bean Soup

This is a marriage of convenience between canned foods and fresh, but it's a fairly passionate soup.

4 strips lean salt pork, diced
1 small onion, thinly sliced
1 clove garlic, minced
1/4 cup celery, finely chopped
1 cup canned kidney beans, drained
1 cup canned Italian tomatoes
4 cups beef broth
1/2 tsp basil
Salt and pepper to taste
1 cup small pasta shells
Garnish: Parmesan cheese & chopped parsley

Saute salt pork in a saucepan until lightly browned. Add onion, garlic and celery. Saute vegetables until tender. Add kidney beans, tomatoes and beef broth. Cover and simmer 20 minutes. Season with basil and salt and pepper to taste. Add pasta shells and simmer another 15 minutes or until pasta is cooked. Spoon soup into bowls and top with a sprinkling of Parmesan cheese and parsley. Makes 4 servings.

Chicken, Rice & Sour Cream Casserole

*There's always one casserole that everybody loves,
and you serve it again and again —
until your old man tells you to knock it off.
This is it.*

3/4 lb Jack cheese
3 cups sour cream
1 tsp salt
4-oz can green chiles, diced
3 cups cooked white rice
1 tsp salt
1/2 tsp pepper
2 cups cooked chicken, diced
3/4 cup Cheddar cheese, grated

Cut cheese into strips. Mix sour cream with salt and drained chiles. Butter a 2-quart casserole. Season cooked rice with salt and pepper. Spoon out a layer of rice over the bottom of the casserole, and top with a layer of sour cream-chile mixture. Place a layer of cheese strips on top, and 1 cup of diced chicken. Repeat layering, reserving enough rice for final topping. Bake in a 350 degree oven for 1/2 hour. Sprinkle with Cheddar cheese, and bake another 10 minutes until cheese melts. This casserole may be made ahead, and baked just before serving. Serves 4.

Won Ton From The Little Red Book

Not from Mao's Little Red Book, but our collection of great thoughts to nourish the inner man — and inner woman.

2 wafer thin pork chops
1 Tbsp peanut oil
1/4 cup boiled ham, finely chopped
1/4 cup green onions, finely chopped
2 Tbsp cilantro parsley,
    finely chopped
1/4 cup water chestnuts, minced
1 Tbsp fresh ginger, grated
1/2 tsp sugar
1 1/2 Tbsp soy sauce
1 egg, beaten
1 small package prepared won ton skins
6 cups chicken broth
1/2 small bunch of spinach

Remove fat from pork chops and cut meat from bone. Dice pork finely. Add oil to skillet and stir fry pork until meat is browned and cooked. Add ham and green onions and stir fry 1 minute longer. Remove skillet from heat. In a bowl combine pork, ham, green onions, cilantro parsley, water chestnuts, ginger, sugar, soy sauce and egg. Blend well. Spoon 1/2 Tbsp of mixture in the center of each won ton skin. Bring top and bottom together over filling. Moisten edges and seal with a squeeze so won ton looks like a little pillow. Bring chicken broth to a simmer and gently drop won ton in, one by one. Simmer 3 minutes. Wash spinach and remove tough stems; cut in 3-inch lengths. Add spinach to soup. Simmer 3 minutes longer. Serve in large soup bowls. Makes 4 servings.

Day Before Payday Soy Grit Tacos

*Suffering negative cash flow? This is your taco!
It tastes as good — or better — than hamburger tacos.*

1 cup soy grits
1 large onion, finely chopped
2 Tbsp margarine
1 1/2 cups water
1/4 cup soy sauce
cornmeal tortillas
1 cup cooking oil
Bean sprouts
Red onion, finely chopped
Avocado, sliced
Shredded Cheddar cheese
Tomatoes, chopped
Mexican hot sauce

Put soy grits in a large pot, and cover grits with 3 inches of water. Soak grits at least 6 hours. Drain. Saute onion in margarine until tender. Combine soy grits, onion, water and soy sauce in pot. Cover and simmer 30 to 40 minutes. Fry tortillas in hot oil a few seconds on each side and fold in half into tacos. Drain tortillas on paper towels. Spoon a few tablespoons of soy grits into each taco, as you would hamburger filling, and add a helping of bean sprouts, red onions, avocado, cheese, tomatoes or whatever garnishes you want. Serve the hot sauce on the side. There are several brands of Mexican hot sauces on the market. We prefer the Ortaga Green Chile Salsa. This recipe makes enough soy grits for tacos for 4 people.

The Second Time Around

If love is better the second time around, so are meat or chicken leftovers when used in savory casseroles.

1 cup white rice
1/4 cup raisins, preferably white
1 1/2 cups cooked meat or chicken, diced
1/4 cup green onions, chopped
1 Tbsp chili powder
1/2 tsp orange or lemon rind, grated
1 tsp garlic powder
10 1/2-oz can consomme
10 1/2-oz can water
Topping: tomato slices

Combine rice, raisins, meat or chicken, green onions, chili powder, orange or lemon rind, garlic powder, consomme and water in a buttered casserole. Top with tomato slices. Cover and bake in a 400 degree oven for 45 minutes to an hour. Do not overcook. Test rice in 45 minutes to see if it's done. Makes 3 to 4 servings.

Chicken Enchiladas

What the world needs now are more chicken enchiladas and less politicians.

2 Tbsp margarine
2 Tbsp flour
1 cup milk
1/2 tsp salt
1/4 tsp pepper
1 small onion, finely chopped
2 garlic cloves, minced

2 Tbsp olive oil
3 oz canned green chile, diced & drained
2 cups cooked chicken, diced
Flour tortillas
Jack cheese, grated
Garnish: sour cream & avocado slices

Melt margarine in skillet, add flour and gradually stir in milk. Stir until sauce thickens. Season with salt and pepper. In a separate skillet, saute onion and garlic in olive oil until tender, and add to sauce. Add chiles and chicken to sauce and cook 1 minute. In a lightly greased skillet, fry tortillas on one side until lightly browned. Spoon a couple of tablespoons of chicken filling on the browned side of each tortilla, and sprinkle with 2 Tbsp of Jack cheese. Bring up the sides of the tortilla, overlap them, and secure with a toothpick. Put enchiladas, seam side up, on a baking sheet. Bake in a preheated 350 degree oven for 20 minutes or until heated through. Serve enchiladas topped with sour cream and garnished with avocado slices. Makes 3 to 4 servings.

French Beans & Lamb Casserole

*The only bean to make the social register is the French bean or haricot,
also known as The Beautiful Peoples' bean.
Here's a budget party dish.*

2 cups small white beans
1 Tbsp salt
1 onion, studded with 2 cloves
1 bay leaf
1 clove garlic
1 cup flour
1 tsp salt
1/2 tsp pepper
2 1/2 lb boneless lamb shoulder,
   cut into 1 1/2 inch cubes
2 Tbsp olive oil
2 small leeks (white part only)
   sliced
1 clove garlic
1 tsp thyme
1 cup beef broth
1 cup red wine
1/4 cup buttered breadcrumbs

Cover beans with water and bring to a boil. Remove from stove and soak beans 1 hour. Drain. Put beans in saucepan with salt, onion, bay leaf and garlic. Add water to cover. Simmer until beans are tender. Drain and put in casserole. Season flour with salt and pepper. Dust lamb in flour, and then brown meat in hot olive oil. Add leeks, garlic, thyme, broth and wine. Simmer until lamb is tender. Combine lamb, leeks and pan juice with beans in casserole. Bake uncovered in a 350 degree oven for 45 to 60 minutes. Baste beans with additional broth and wine, if needed, to keep beans moist and mellow. Sprinkle breadcrumbs over top the last 15 minutes of baking. Serves 6.

Lazy Lasagne

In the Mafia, they'd shoot you for using a spaghetti sauce mix, but it's an easy way to whip up a great lasagne.

1 lb ground round
1 lb 12-oz can Italian plum tomatoes
8-oz can tomato sauce
3-oz package spaghetti sauce mix
2 cloves garlic, minced
Salt to taste
8-oz package lasagne noodles
8-oz Mozzarella cheese, sliced
1 cup cream style cottage cheese
1/2 cup Parmesan cheese, grated

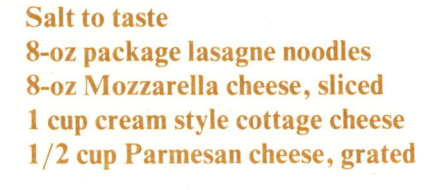

Brown meat and drain fat. Add tomatoes, tomato sauce, spaghetti sauce mix and garlic. Cover and simmer 40 minutes stirring occasionally. Salt to taste. Cook noodles in boiling, salted water according to directions on package. Drain; rinse noodles in cold water. Place half the noodles in a rectangular baking dish. Cover with 1/3 of the sauce. Layer 1/2 the Mozzarella cheese and 1/2 the cottage cheese over the top. Repeat layering, ending with the sauce on top. Sprinkle Parmesan cheese over top. Bake in a 350 oven for 25 minutes. Let stand 10 minutes before cutting into serving squares. Makes 4 to 6 servings.

Honey Marmalade Nut Bread

As good as it sounds. Maybe better.

**2 1/2 cups white flour
1 Tbsp baking powder
1 tsp salt
1/2 cup orange honey
2 Tbsp margarine
3 eggs, beaten
1 cup orange marmalade
1 Tbsp grated orange peel
1 cup walnuts or pecans,
   finely chopped**

Sift together flour, baking powder and salt. In a separate bowl, beat together honey, margarine and eggs. Stir in orange marmalade and grated orange peel. Combine with flour mixture and blend well. Stir in walnuts or pecans, which have been dusted with flour. Pour into greased loaf pan. Bake 1 hour in preheated 350 degree oven. Cool in pan 10 minutes before removing.

Sunday Thru Tuesday Pot Roast

A pot roast lasts just long enough to give you several different meals, but not long enough to bore you. A perfect houseguest.

4-lb pot roast
2 Tbsp cooking oil
6 small boiling onions, peeled
3 small carrots, quartered
1/2 cup celery, chopped
1/2 cup green pepper, finely chopped
1 clove garlic
1 tsp salt
1/2 tsp pepper
1/2 tsp thyme
1 bay leaf
1 Tbsp parsley
2/3 cup red wine

Brown roast in hot oil. Place meat in the center of a sufficiently large sheet of heavy duty foil to enclose meat and the following vegetables: onions, carrots, celery, green pepper and garlic. Season roast with salt, pepper, thyme, bay leaf and parsley. Bring up sides of foil around the meat to make a container, and pour in red wine. Seal foil on top with a tight double fold. Place in pan and roast meat in a 325 oven for 3 1/2 hours, or until meat is fork tender. Serve with natural gravy and vegetables. Makes 6 servings.

Fresh Lemon Loaf

When checks bounce, bills pile and kids scream, the happy homemaker needs a little ambrosia to remind her that life is sweet.

1/2 cup margarine
1 cup sugar
2 eggs, beaten
1 2/3 cup white flour
1 tsp baking powder
1 tsp salt
1/2 cup milk
1/2 cup walnuts, chopped
2 Tbsp lemon peel, grated
Juice of 1 lemon, strained
1/4 cup sugar

Cream together margarine and sugar; beat in eggs. In a separate bowl, sift flour with baking powder and salt. Add flour mixture and milk alternately to margarine-sugar mixture, then beat well. Stir in chopped walnuts, lightly dusted with flour, and lemon peel. Pour into greased loaf pan, and bake in a preheated 350 degree oven for 1 hour. Remove. Combine lemon juice with sugar and pour over the top of the hot lemon loaf. Cool — and have a slice!

Chapter II

Living Together on Love and Vegetables

Since the first lovers were vegetarians, this chapter is dedicated to you loving herbivores who share bed, board and beans together. While living together on love and vegetables is nothing you can write home about, it's a lifestyle fortified with natural vitamins. On the following pages are inventive ways to prepare grain and greenery so they're as delicious as they are nutritious. When used as a main course, portions for four serve two.

Tarzan & Jane's Raw Vegetable Surprise

From Tarzan and Jane, the world's first swingers, comes a wild idea for a raw vegetable sandwich.

3 Tbsp minced cabbage
3 Tbsp minced carrots
3 Tbsp minced green pepper
3 Tbsp minced celery
3 Tbsp minced radishes
3 Tbsp minced red onion
1 1/2 cups Cheddar cheese, grated
4 Tbsp beer
White pepper and Cayenne to taste
2 slices buttered toast

Combine raw vegetables in a bowl. Spoon out 1/2 cup of the vegetables on each piece of toast. In a double broiler, stir cheese and beer together, and heat cheese until it melts. Season cheese sauce with white pepper and cayenne to taste. Put toast on a baking sheet. Spoon cheese sauce equally over the vegetables. Broil sandwiches for 3 minutes or until cheese lightly browns. Serves 2.

The Health Nut's Nut Loaf 24

If you're nesting with a health freak, here's a tasty way you both can enjoy his wheat germ.

1 1/2 cups celery, minced
1/2 cup onions, minced
1/4 cup green pepper, minced
1/2 cup margarine
2 cups cooked rice
1 1/2 cups pecans, chopped
1 cup wheat germ
2 Tbsp pimiento, chopped
1 tsp salt
1/4 tsp pepper
4 eggs, beaten

Saute celery, onions and green pepper in margarine until tender. Combine with rice, pecans, wheat germ, pimiento, salt, pepper and eggs. Mix well. Pack into greased 9 x 5 x 3 loaf pan. Bake in a 375 oven for 40 to 45 minutes. Let loaf stand in pan 5 minutes before removing. Makes 6 servings.

Spinach Gnocchi

Lovers need all the iron they can get.

**10-oz package frozen chopped spinach
2 Tbsp margarine
2 Tbsp flour
1 cup milk
1/2 tsp salt
1/3 cup Parmesan cheese
1 egg, beaten
1 egg yolk, beaten
3/4 cup flour
2 qts salted water
Melted margarine
Parmesan cheese**

Cook spinach according to directions on package. Press out all excess water with a slotted spoon. Melt margarine in skillet and stir in flour. Gradually add milk and stir until sauce thickens. Season with salt. Add Parmesan cheese and cook until sauce is smooth. Combine egg and egg yolk in a bowl and stir a little white sauce into eggs, then stir eggs back into white sauce. Add spinach to sauce, stir and cool. Blend 1/2 cup flour into creamed spinach. With a spoon shape spinach into small dumplings and roll dumplings on a pastry board sprinkled with 1/4 cup flour. Bring 2 qts salted water to a simmer. Drop spinach dumplings, one at a time, into simmering, but not boiling water. When dumplings rise to surface, remove with slotted spoon. Arrange on platter and drizzle with a generous amount of margarine and Parmesan cheese. Makes 4 servings.

Minestrone Genovese

Minestrone Genovese is a production as long as an Italian opera, but it's a beautiful party soup.

2 cups white beans
1 Tbsp salt
3 Tbsp olive oil
1/2 cup onion, finely chopped
2 cups eggplant, diced
1/2 cup mushrooms, finely chopped
4 cups cabbage, shredded
2 cups zucchini, sliced
2 cups canned Italian tomatoes
1/2 tsp pepper
2 tsp salt
2 1/2 qts boiling water
1/2 cup vermicelli
1/4 cup parsley, minced
2 cloves garlic, minced
1/3 cup blanched almonds
1/3 cup grated Parmesan cheese
1/2 tsp basil
3 Tbsp olive oil

Cover beans with water, bring to a boil and remove from heat. Soak beans 1 hour. Drain. Cover beans with more water, add salt and simmer beans until tender. Heat olive oil in skillet and saute onions until golden. Add eggplant, mushrooms, cabbage, zucchini, tomatoes, pepper and salt. Simmer 5 minutes. Combine vegetables with cooked beans and 2 1/2 qts boiling water. Simmer over low heat 30 minutes. Correct seasoning adding more salt if necessary. Add vermicelli and cook until pasta is tender, about 10 minutes. In a blender or mortar, combine parsley, garlic, almonds, cheese and basil. Blend until a paste or pesto forms, gradually adding the olive oil. Just before serving, stir the pesto slowly into the soup so it does not lump. Serves 8 to 10.

Russian Eggplant

A Russian eggplant with equal amounts of sour cream and soul to make your meaningful relationship more meaningful.

1 eggplant
1/2 cup flour
1/4 cup cooking oil
1 tsp salt
4 Tbsp margarine
2 Tbsp flour
2 cups sour cream
1/2 cup cooked, sauteed mushrooms
3 Tbsp Parmesan cheese
Garnish: paprika

Peel eggplant and cut into 1-inch slices. Dip eggplant into flour. Heat a few tablespoons of cooking oil at a time, and saute eggplant slices until golden brown. Sprinkle with salt. In another skillet heat margarine and stir in flour. Slowly add sour cream and stir until hot. Place 1 layer of eggplant slices in a buttered casserole. Spoon over sauteed mushrooms. Cover mushrooms with half of the sour cream. Top with another layer of eggplant slices, and spoon over remaining sour cream. Sprinkle with cheese and garnish with paprika. Run under broiler to brown. Makes 4 servings.

Barley Bowl with Mushrooms

*Barley is very nutritious—ask any Scotch drinker.
Here the pearly grain is combined with fresh mushrooms.*

1/2 cups onions, minced
3 Tbsp margarine
1 cup uncooked pearl barley
3 cups consomme

1/2 lb mushrooms, sliced
1 Tbsp margarine
Salt & pepper & garlic powder to taste

Saute onions in margarine until golden. Stir in barley and cook over low heat until barley begins to brown. Transfer onions and barley to a casserole, and pour in consomme. Cover and bake in a 350 degree oven until barley has absorbed liquid and is tender, in about 1 hour. Saute mushrooms in margarine until tender. Season with salt, pepper and garlic powder to taste. Add mushrooms to barley before serving. Makes 4 servings.

Dr. Fu Manchu's Chinese Stir-Fry

That cunning genius, Dr. Fu Manchu, discovered that broccoli is quicker to cook in a stir-fry if you parboil it first.

1/2 lb broccoli, broken into flowerets
3 Tbsp peanut oil
6 water chestnuts, sliced
7-oz can mushrooms, sliced
1/3 cup chicken stock
1 Tbsp sherry
2 Tbsp soy sauce
2 tsp cornstarch
1 tsp sesame oil

Cut broccoli flowerets in half lengthwise. Drop broccoli in boiling, salted water and parboil 1 1/2 minutes. Drain. Heat peanut oil in wok or skillet, and stir-fry water chestnuts and mushrooms 1 minute. Add chicken stock, sherry, soy sauce, cornstarch and sesame oil and simmer 1 minute. Add broccoli and stir-fry another 2 minutes. Makes 4 servings.

Bean & Green Salad

This has always been a man's salad -- lusty, hearty and full of beans. Now, thanks to the Equal Rights Amendment, you can enjoy it too.

1/2 cup cauliflower, broken into flowerets
1 head red lettuce
1 cup curly endive
1/2 cup cooked green beans
1/2 cup canned red kidney beans, drained
1/2 cup canned garbanzos, drained

4 Tbsp green onions, sliced
1 hard-cooked egg, chopped
4 Tbsp olive oil
2 Tbsp wine winegar
1/2 tsp dry mustard
1/2 tsp salt
1/2 tsp pepper
Garnish: sliced tomatoes & sliced black olives

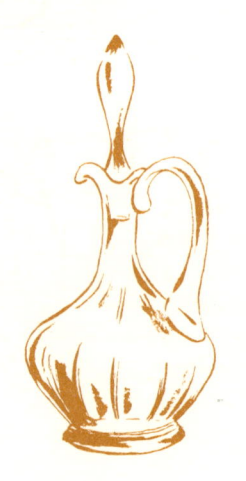

Steam cauliflower 5 minutes until barely tender. Break lettuce and endive into bite-size pieces. Combine greens in a large salad bowl with green beans, kidney beans, garbanzos, green onions, cauliflower and chopped egg. Mix together salad dressing of olive oil, wine vinegar, mustard, salt and pepper. Just before serving, toss salad with dressing, and garnish with tomatoes and black olives. 4 servings.

Honey Walnut Bread

Living on love and vegetables is not enough if you don't have a crust of homemade bread to eat.

1 cup milk
1 cup honey
1/4 cup soft margarine
2 1/2 cups whole wheat flour
2 eggs, beaten
1 tsp salt
1 Tbsp baking powder
1/2 cup walnuts, chopped

Combine milk and honey in a saucepan and heat until blended. Pour into a bowl and beat in margarine, whole wheat flour, eggs, salt and baking powder. Fold in walnuts which have been dusted with flour. Pour into a greased loaf pan. Bake in a preheated 325 degree oven for 1 hour. Cool 15 minutes in pan before removing.

A Broccoli Spectacular

Spectacular enough for those formal vegetarian dinners when it's strictly white tie and T-shirt.

1 1/2 lbs broccoli
3 cups cottage cheese
3 eggs
6 Tbsp margarine, softened
1/3 cup flour
1/4 cup onion, finely minced
8-oz can whole kernel corn, drained
1/2 lb Cheddar or Swiss cheese, diced
1/2 tsp salt
1/4 tsp pepper
Dash of Tabasco sauce
2 Tbsp margarine
1/2 cup soft breadcrumbs
1/2 cup Cheddar cheese, shredded

Remove tough parts of the broccoli stalks. Steam broccoli until crisp tender. Chop finely. In a blender, combine cottage cheese, eggs, margarine and flour. Blend until mixture is smooth and creamy. Fold in broccoli, onion, corn, Cheddar or Swiss cheese, salt, pepper and Tabasco. Pour mixture into a greased, deep 2 1/2 qt casserole. Melt 2 Tbsp margarine and saute fresh breadcrumbs until golden brown. Sprinkle over casserole along with a topping of Cheddar cheese. Bake 1 hour in a 350 degree oven until casserole is firm. Serves 6 to 8.

Curried Green Beans

*Love is never having to say you're sorry . . .
for serving vegetable platitudes.*

**2 cups green beans,
 broken into 2-inch lengths
1/2 cup celery, sliced
1/4 cup green onions, sliced
2 Tbsp margarine
1/2 cup water chestnuts, sliced
1/4 cup sour cream
1/4 cup mayonnaise
1 1/2 tsp curry powder
1/2 tsp salt
1/4 tsp pepper**

Steam beans until barely tender. Saute celery and green onions in margarine for a few minutes. Combine beans, celery, onions and water chestnuts in a casserole. Blend together sour cream, mayonnaise, curry powder, salt and pepper. Stir into casserole. Bake in a 300 degree oven until hot. Makes 4 servings.

Muffled Carrot Muffins

*You can munch these carrot muffins without making a sound.
Perfect for eating in bed.*

1/4 cup margarine
1/4 cup brown sugar
2 eggs, beaten
1 Tbsp lemon juice
1 Tbsp water
1 cup finely shredded carrots, lightly packed
1 cup white flour
2 tsp baking powder
1/2 tsp ginger
1/2 tsp salt
1/2 cup walnuts, chopped

Beat together margarine with sugar. Stir in eggs, lemon juice, water and shredded carrots. In a separate bowl, mix together flour, baking powder, ginger and salt. Sift flour mixture into carrot mixture; add walnuts, which have been dusted with flour. Stir just long enough to moisten ingredients. Grease 12 muffin pans, and fill each 2/3 full. Bake in a preheated 400 degree oven for 20 minutes until muffins are golden brown.

Zuper Zucchini

For liberated lovers, an unconventional zucchini that dares to be different. It's sliced lengthwise.

3/4 cup sour cream
1 Tbsp tarragon vinegar
2 egg yolks, beaten
1/2 tsp paprika
6 zucchini
1/2 tsp salt

Blend together sour cream, tarragon vinegar, egg yolks and paprika. Pour into the top of a double boiler over hot, but not boiling water. Stir sauce until it thickens. Cut tips off zucchini and slice zucchini lengthwise in very thin slices. Steam vegetable until tender, about 5 minutes. Season with salt. Spoon sour cream sauce over zucchini before serving. Serves 4.

Baked Acorn Squash with Pineapple

Can a vegetable and fruit from two different worlds find happiness together? Decidedly.

2 acorn squashes
4 tsp dry sherry
4 tsp brown sugar
4 tsp margarine
2 Tbsp margarine
1/2 cup canned crushed pineapple, drained
1/4 tsp nutmeg
1 tsp salt

Cut squash in half lengthwise, and scoop out seeds and fibers. Place on greased baking dish. Into each squash cavity, spoon 1 tsp dry sherry, 1 tsp brown sugar and 1 tsp margarine. Cover and bake in a 400 degree oven for 30 minutes or until tender. Scoop out cooked squash, leaving a 1/4 inch shell. Mix squash with margarine, and pineapple and season with nutmeg and salt. Spoon mixture equally back into shells. Bake for 15 minutes longer in a 350 degree oven. Serves 4.

Four Ways To Get Sauced

Lemon Cheese Sauce

Combine 1/4 cup melted margarine or butter with 2 Tbsp grated lemon rind, 1 tsp salt, 1/2 tsp cracked pepper, 2 Tbsp chopped parsley and 1/4 cup grated Gruyere or Swiss cheese. Spoon sauce over hot, steamed vegetables and toss until cheese melts a little. Especially good on green beans, carrots and squash.

Yogurt Sauce

Melt 1 Tbsp butter or margarine and stir in 1 1/2 Tbsp flour, 1/4 tsp salt and a dash of cayenne. Gradually stir in 1/2 cup milk and cook until it thickens. Carefully stir white sauce into 1/2 cup plain yogurt. Return to stove and heat until sauce is hot. Try this over broccoli, asparagus, green beans, cabbage, or any vegetable you like.

Piquant Vegetable Sauce

In the top of a double boiler, combine 1/4 tsp dry mustard, 3/4 tsp salt, 1 tsp sugar, 1/4 tsp paprika, 1 beaten egg, 1/4 cup tarragon vinegar or lemon juice, and 2 Tbsp olive oil. Heat sauce until it thickens and stir in 1 Tbsp melted butter, 1/4 tsp curry powder and 1/2 tsp grated onion. Great over cabbage, cauliflower or green beans.

Green Onion Sauce

Beat 1/3 cup of softened butter until fluffy. Gradually add 2 Tbsp lemon juice and season with 1/4 tsp salt, 1/4 tsp paprika. Add 2 Tbsp minced green onions and 1/2 Tbsp minced parsley. Nifty over carrots, peas, green beans, and asparagus.

Chapter III

Slow Cookery and Fast Meals for the Working Couple

The hard day at the office is no longer a male prerogative. The working wife also enjoys a hard day at the office. In theory, working couples share the cooking and marketing chores — but like all theories, don't count on it. The working wife must be prepared to man the stove with meals that stir up in minutes — or better yet, dinners that cook themselves in the electric crock pot. This chapter covers both. If you're married to a man who can't cook, let him push the button on the crock pot, so he'll feel like he's role-sharing.

Curried Lamb

A slow cooker that serves you a delectable curried lamb at the end of the day is better than a faithful Indian servant. You don't have to pay the cooker.

4 Tbsp margarine
1 clove garlic, minced
2 small onions, sliced
2 lbs boneless lamb shoulder, cut in 2-inch pieces
1/2 cup flour
2 apples, pared & chopped
2 Tbsp curry powder

2 Tbsp brown sugar
3 Tbsp raisins
1 Tbsp Worcestershire sauce
1 small lemon, sliced
1/3 cup walnuts, chopped
1 tsp salt
2 cups water

Melt margarine in skillet and saute garlic and onions until golden. Remove from skillet. Dust lamb with flour and brown in skillet. Add apples and curry powder, and stir and simmer for 5 minutes. Transfer garlic, onions, lamb and apple-curry mixture to slow cooker. Season meat with brown sugar, raisins, Worcestershire sauce, lemon, walnuts and salt. Add water. Cover and cook on low heat for 8 to 10 hours. (Regular cooking time 1 1/2 hours.) Serve over rice. Makes 4 servings.

Lentil Soup

After a day of winning through intimidation, you can use a thick, nourishing soup.

1/4 cup cooking oil
3 cups cooked ham, diced
1/2 lb Polish sausage, cut in 1/2 inch slices
2 large onions, chopped
1 clove garlic, crushed
2 cups celery with leaves, chopped
1 large peeled tomato, quartered
1 lb lentils, rinsed in cold water
3 qts water
1/2 tsp Tabasco
1 Tbsp salt
1/2 bunch fresh spinach leaves, washed

Heat oil in skillet and add ham, sausage, onions and garlic, Saute for 5 minutes. Put meat and vegetables in slow cooker with celery, tomato, lentils, water, Tabasco and salt. Remove tough stems from spinach and cut spinach into bite sized pieces. Add to pot. Cover and cook on low heat for 8 to 10 hours. (Regular cooking time 2 hours.) Makes 4 qts.

A John Wayne Turkey

From out of the West, barbecue turkey for cowboys and schoolmarms, gamblers and dance hall girls — or any working couple.

1/4 cup onions, chopped
1 Tbsp margarine
1/3 cup water
1 cup chili sauce
2 Tbsp cider vinegar
1 Tbsp Worcestershire sauce
1/4 cup lemon juice
2 Tbsp brown sugar
1 tsp salt
1/4 tsp paprika
Dash of Tabasco
2 turkey drumsticks
1/3 cup water

Saute onions in margarine until lightly browned. Add water, chili sauce, vinegar, Worcestershire sauce, lemon juice, brown sugar, salt, paprika and Tabasco. Simmer for 15 minutes, stirring frequently. Place drumsticks in slow cooker and pour barbecue sauce over top. Add 1/3 cup of water in the bottom of cooker. Cover and cook on low heat for 8 to 10 hours. (Regular cooking time 2 hours.) 4 servings.

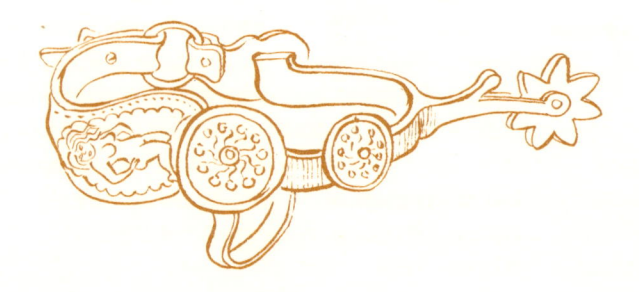

The Best Beef Stew ~~No Good~~

Good stews, like good men, are hard to find.

2 lbs beef chuck, cut into
    1 inch pieces
3 Tbsp margarine
6 small white boiling onions, peeled
3 carrots, sliced
1/2 lb mushrooms, sliced
1 clove garlic, minced
1 small can tomato paste
2 Tbsp parsley, chopped
2 Tbsp flour
1 tsp salt
1/2 tsp pepper
1 bay leaf, crushed
1/2 tsp each rosemary, basil & oregano
2 cups red wine
Garnish: sour cream

Melt margarine and brown meat in skillet. Transfer meat to slow cooker. Lightly brown onions, carrots and mushrooms and garlic in skillet. Stir in tomato paste, parsley and flour and blend until smooth. Combine vegetable-tomato mixture with meat in the slow cooker. Season with salt, pepper, bay leaf, rosemary, basil and oregano. Pour in red wine. Cover and cook at low heat 8 to 10 hours. (Regular cooking time 2 hours.) Garnish stew with a dollop of sour cream before serving. Makes 4 servings.

Dinner Omelet

The French created the omelet for tired working couples who have just enough energy to whip up one of the great dishes of the world.

2 Tbsp margarine
1 tomato, peeled and chopped
2 green onions, finely chopped
1/3 cup mushrooms, sliced
1/4 cup boiled ham, chopped
1/2 tsp basil
1/2 tsp salt
4 egg whites
4 egg yolks
4 Tbsp sour cream
1/4 cup Cheddar cheese, shredded

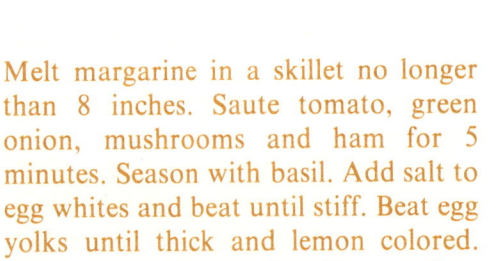

Melt margarine in a skillet no longer than 8 inches. Saute tomato, green onion, mushrooms and ham for 5 minutes. Season with basil. Add salt to egg whites and beat until stiff. Beat egg yolks until thick and lemon colored. Fold egg whites and yolks together. Fold in sour cream, cheese and vegetable-ham mixture. Pour into lightly greased skillet. Cook over low heat for 3 or 4 minutes until omelet is lightly browned on the bottom, then run skillet under the broiler. Cook until omelet is puffy and golden brown on top. Cut omelet in half and serve on warm plates, please. Serves 2.

Chicken Soup That Mother Never Made

*If one of your hang-ups is a mother that never made you chicken soup,
here's the soup that mother never made —
simmered with the help of your motherly cooker.*

3 Tbsp margarine
1 cup celery, diced
1/2 cup leeks (white part only) sliced
1 onion, finely chopped
1 broiler-fryer, cut in small sections
1 1/2 tsp salt
1 Tbsp parsley, chopped
1 bay leaf
1/2 tsp thyme
1/2 tsp pepper
6 cups water
4 Tbsp margarine
4 Tbsp flour
2 egg yolks, beaten
3 Tbsp lemon juice
Garnish: lemon slices & minced parsley

Melt margarine in skillet and saute celery, leeks and onions until soft, but not browned. Transfer vegetables to slow cooker and add chicken pieces. Season with salt, parsley, bay leaf, thyme and pepper. Add water. Cover and cook at low heat 8 to 10 hours. (Regular cooking time 1 hour, 15 min.) Remove chicken and keep warm. Melt margarine in a skillet, stir in flour. Gradually pour in 4 cups of chicken stock from slow cooker. Stir until stock thickens and return to cooker. Beat egg yolks lightly with lemon juice; add a little hot stock and stir eggs back into cooker. Remove immediately from heat. Place chicken pieces in large soup bowls and pour thickened soup stock over them. Garnish with lemon slices and parsley. Serve with knife, fork and soup spoon. Makes 4 servings.

New Mexico Green Chile Chili

This chili won't make you cry, but it's hot enough to make you whistle.

2 Tbsp cooking oil
2 lbs beef chuck, cut into cubes
1/2 tsp salt
2 onions, chopped
2 cloves garlic, minced
1 lb 12-oz can tomatoes
1 lb can tomatoes
7-oz can green chiles, diced & drained
2 1-lb cans kidney beans, undrained
1-lb can yellow hominy, drained
2 cups water
2 tsp beef stock base or
    2 cubes beef bouillon

Heat oil and quickly brown meat. Season with salt. Add onions and garlic and stir until golden. Transfer meat, onions and garlic to slow cooker. Mash tomatoes into small pieces with a fork, and add to cooker, along with green chiles, kidney beans, hominy, water and beef stock base or bouillon cubes. Cover and cook at low heat for 8 to 10 hours. (Regular cooking time 2 1/2 hours.) Add more salt, if desired, before serving. Makes 4 to 6 servings.

Avocado Stuffed with Salmon Salad

When it's his week to cook, here's a simple salad he can't ruin unless the electric can opener blows a fuse.

2 small, ripe avocadoes
1/3 cup mayonnaise
1 Tbsp lemon juice
1 Tbsp chili sauce
1/4 tsp salt
7 3/4-oz can salmon, drained
3 Tbsp celery, finely chopped
3 Tbsp green onions, finely chopped
Garnish: chopped egg & paprika

Cut avocadoes in half and remove pit. In a bowl, mix together mayonnaise, lemon juice, chili sauce and salt. Flake salmon; remove skin and bones. Combine salmon with celery and green onions. Mix with dressing, and spoon salmon into avocado halves. Garnish with chopped egg and paprika. Serves 2.

Mediterranean Lamb Shanks & Vegetables

A traditional lamb and vegetable casserole from the Mediterranean—where every man is a lover—except on Sunday when he's a soccer player.

2 tomatoes, peeled, seeded & quartered
1/2 cup zucchini, sliced
1/2 cup eggplant, peeled & diced
1/2 cup mushrooms, cut in half
2 Tbsp margarine
2 lamb shanks
1 clove garlic, minced

1/4 tsp thyme
1/4 tsp basil
1 tsp salt
1/2 tsp pepper
1 Tbsp parsley
1 bay leaf
1/2 cup beef broth

Combine tomatoes, zucchini, eggplant and mushrooms in the bottom of the slow cooker. Melt margarine in a skillet and brown lamb shanks. Place lamb over the vegetables in the cooker and season with garlic, thyme, basil, salt, pepper, and parsley. Add bay leaf and pour in beef broth. Cover and cook on low heat for 8 to 10 hours. (Regular cooking time 3 hours.) 2 servings.

Abie's Irish Corned Beef

*As Irish as corned beef and cabbage, and Jewish as corned beef on rye,
this lovable brisket is all things to all people.
It oughta run for office.*

4-lb corned beef brisket
2 oranges, thinly sliced
1 lemon, thinly sliced
1 bay leaf
2 small onions, sliced
1/4 cup brown sugar
1 Tbsp pickling spices

Place brisket in slow cooker; cover with cold water. Add oranges, lemons, bay leaf, onions, brown sugar and pickling spices. Cover and cook at low heat 10 to 12 hours. (Regular cooking time 4 hours.) Makes 6 servings.

Rice and....

A savory casserole that takes on any leftovers — chicken, meat or shellfish. But please, no hot dogs. This dish may be humble, but it's proud.

1 small onion, chopped
2 Tbsp long green chile pepper or bell pepper
3 Tbsp olive oil
1 cup white rice
1 lb 12-oz can tomatoes, drained
1/2 cup tomato liquid from can
1 1/2 cups water
1/2 tsp salt
1/2 tsp garlic salt
1 1/2 cups cooked, diced chicken, meat or shellfish
1 cup Cheddar cheese, grated

Saute onion and green pepper or bell pepper in olive oil until tender. Add rice and saute another few minutes until rice is golden. Add tomatoes, tomato liquid, water, salt, garlic salt, and chicken, meat or shellfish. Cover and simmer until rice is tender. Before serving sprinkle cheese over rice. Makes 3 to 4 servings.

Zucchini Bread

The working couples' bread. He chops, she stirs, he beats, she sifts, and together they bake a wonderfully tasty bread that's slightly sweet and spicy. What a nice way to eat your vegetables.

3 eggs, beaten
2 cups sugar
1 cup vegetable oil
1 Tbsp vanilla
2 cups coarsely grated zucchini
2 cups flour
2 tsp baking soda
1 Tbsp cinnamon
1 tsp salt
1/4 tsp baking powder
1 cup walnuts, chopped

In a bowl, beat together eggs with sugar, vegetable oil and vanilla. Beat mixture until it is thick and lemon colored. Stir in zucchini, which should be coarsely packed in measuring cup. Sift flour with baking soda, cinnamon, salt and baking powder. Combine with egg-zucchini mixture. Fold in walnuts, which have been dusted with flour. Pour mixture into 2 greased and floured loaf pans. Bake in a preheated 350 degree oven for 1 hour. Cool bread in pans for 10 minutes before inverting onto rack to cool completely. Makes 2 loaves, one for each of you.

Velly Fast Chinese Chicken Salad

The Chinese were making chicken salad 4,000 years before the American club woman. Practice makes perfect.

1/2 cup bean threads (sai fun)
Cooking Oil
1 1/2 cups cooked, boned chicken, cut in strips
1/2 head iceberg lettuce, shredded lengthwise
1/4 cup toasted almonds, chopped
2 Tbsp sesame seeds, toasted
1 Tbsp sugar
1/2 tsp pepper
1/2 tsp salt
1/4 cup salad oil
Dash of sesame oil (optional)
3 Tbsp white vinegar
1/3 cup cilantro parsley, chopped

Drop bean threads into hot cooking oil, and stir constantly for a few seconds until bean threads are crisp and lightly browned. Remove from skillet. In a large salad bowl, combine bean threads, chicken, lettuce, almonds and sesame seeds. Make a dressing of sugar, pepper, salt, salad oil, sesame oil, (if desired), and white vinegar. Toss salad with dressing and sprinkle cilanto parsley over top. Makes 2 servings.

Peso-Pinchers

*When it's survival time to payday, give thanks to the bandito
who invented the bean burrito. He was also overdrawn at the bank.*

1 1/3 cups canned refried beans
4 flour tortillas
1 1/2 cups Jack cheese or
    Cheddar cheese, shredded
1 avocado, thinly sliced
4 Tbsp Mexican green chile sauce
4 Tbsp sour cream

Heat beans and spoon 1/3 cup of beans along the center of each tortilla. Top with 1/4 cup of cheese, 1 Tbsp green chile sauce and several slices of avocado. Roll up tortilla and tuck in ends. Place in a shallow baking dish. Sprinkle tortillas with remaining 1/2 cup of cheese. Bake in a 350 degree oven for 10 minutes, or until ingredients are heated through. Garnish tortillas with sour cream before serving.

The Friday Night Bird

Friday night! Time to celebrate your survival in the corporate jungle with a warm bird and a cold bottle.

1 small roasting chicken
1/2 tsp salt
1/2 small onion, peeled
1/3 cup margarine
1 clove garlic, crushed
Juice of 1/2 lemon
Juice of 1/2 orange
1/4 cup sherry
1/2 tsp salt
1/4 tsp pepper
1 tsp rosemary
1/2 tsp tarragon

Rinse chicken with water and pat dry with paper towel. Remove all excess fat from cavity. Salt cavity and place onion inside. Melt margarine and combine with garlic. Brush chicken with margarine-garlic mixture. Place chicken in slow cooker and spoon over lemon juice, orange juice and sherry. Season with salt, pepper, rosemary and tarragon. Cover and cook on low heat 8 to 10 hours. (Regular cooking time 1 1/2 hours.) Makes 4 servings.

Chapter IV

The Singles Scene

The most popular lifestyle today is young, single and carefree. Being single however, isn't all Cloud Nine. It's also being a breadwinner, budget balancer, and in some cases, head of a household. This chapter covers all aspects of singles cookery from mini meals for one to romantic dinners for two. We also include trauma-free, make-ahead parties for the single hostess. And for single parents with small fry, there are tasty recipes that span the generation gap.

Meals with but a Single Thought

> *When you live alone and like it, one of the reasons is the simplicity of dining. No candelabras on the table, no gold service or damask tablecloth, nothing but you and a simple meal. No reason, though, the simple meal can't be a mini-feast!*

The Ten-Minute French Onion Soup

Melt 2 Tbsp margarine in skillet and add 1 large, thinly sliced onion. Saute onion until golden. Add 2 Tbsp dry sherry and a 10 1/2-oz can of consomme. Simmer 10 minutes. Add salt & pepper to taste. Pour into fireproof soup bowl. Top with a slice of French bread. Sprinkle bread liberally with grated Swiss cheese. Run bowl under broiler to melt cheese and toast bread.

Stuffed Baked Potato

Use a large baking potato. Rinse potato in cold water and oil the skin. Bake in a 400 degree oven until tender. Cut off the top of the potato and scoop out the meat leaving a 1/4 inch shell. Whip potato with 1/4 cup sour cream, and 1 Tbsp margarine, and then add 2 Tbsp chopped green onions, 1/2 small tomato, peeled and chopped, 2 Tbsp canned sliced mushrooms, 1 tsp parsley and salt & pepper to taste. Spoon mixture back into potato shell, sprinkle with Cheddar cheese, and bake in oven until cheese melts and potato is hot.

Mexican Green Beans

Snip ends off of 1/2 lb of fresh green beans, leaving the beans whole. Steam until crisp-tender. Salt to taste. Spoon 2 Tbsp of Mexican green chile sauce over beans. Sprinkle liberally with dry breadcrumbs and grated Cheddar cheese. Run under broiler until cheese melts.

Scrambled Eggs and . . . .

Beat together 2 eggs and lightly salt. Add any of the following ingredients, separately or in any combination you like: sauted onions; tomatoes, ham; crisp, crumbled bacon; grated cheese, chipped beef;

mushrooms, crab; shrimp, chile peppers; smoked salmon; cottage cheese, sausages, cream cheese, sour cream, fresh pineapple cubes, cooked vegetables, parsley or curry powder. Melt 1 Tbsp margarine in skillet and pour in eggs. Cook over *low* heat, gently stirring eggs until they are cooked and fluffy, but still moist.

Summer Fruit Salad

Stir together 1/3 cup sour cream, 2 Tbsp honey, 1 Tbsp lime juice, 1/2 tsp grated lime or lemon peel and a dash of salt. Spoon this sublime dressing over a salad of mixed summer fruits; bananas, peaches, apples, pears, pineapple, berries — take your pick!

El Hamburger

Season 1/4 lb of ground round with salt & pepper to taste. Add 1 or 2 Tbsp of red wine (optional), and 2 Tbsp finely chopped green onions. Divide meat into 2 patties. On one patty put a chunk of Jack cheese and 1 tsp diced, canned green chiles. Cover with other patty, pressing edges of meat together. Broil on both sides until done to individual taste.

Cottage Cheese Mix

Before you pack up your thong for a Club Mediterranean vacation, remember that Body English is the principal language of these bikini paradises. Shape up — before you ship out — with low calorie salads like this cottage cheese-vegetable combo. Mix together 1 cup cream cottage cheese, 1/2 tomato peeled and diced, 2 Tbsp diced cucumber, 2 Tbsp diced celery, 1 thinly sliced radish, 1/4 cup diced water chestnuts, 2 Tbsp chopped green onions, and salt & pepper to taste.

Diet Chicken

Another weight-watcher — and delicious!
Brush 1 chicken breast on both sides with lemon juice, and season liberally with salt & pepper, 1/4 tsp rosemary and 1/4 tsp tarragon. Place chicken, rib side up, in a shallow pan and broil quickly for 5 minutes until brown. Turn chicken, skin side up, and place in the bottom of a pan with 3/4-inch boiling water. Bake chicken in a very hot oven, 480 degrees, until fowl is tender and skin is brown and crisp.

Knife & Fork Sandwiches

> Open sandwiches are like open marriages — anything goes! These knife & fork mini-meals are made with one slice of bread and layered with cheeses, meats, vegetables or whatever. "Whatever" is always a handy sandwich to make — just look in the fridge.

Danish Salmon Sandwich

Butter one slice of whole wheat bread and cover with a leaf of Boston lettuce. Mix together 1/3 cup canned salmon (drained and flaked) with 3 Tbsp mayonnaise, 1 Tbsp lemon juice, 1 tsp dill weed and 1 Tbsp chopped green onions. Spoon over lettuce. Garnish with thinly sliced, salted cucumbers. Tuna may be substituted for the salmon.

Cream Cheese Special

Spread a layer of cream cheese over a slice of rye bread. Alternate, in overlaping fashion, thin slices of tomatoes and cucumbers. Spoon over 1 Tbsp of French dressing, and sprinkle with chopped parsley.

Apple, Cheese & Walnut

Lightly butter a slice of dark bread. Cover with thin slices of Cheddar or Jack cheese. Top with thin slices of unpeeled, crisp apple. Sprinkle with finely chopped walnuts.

Salad Sandwich

Place 3 slices of tomato on a slice of toasted whole wheat bread. Spoon 3 Tbsp of cottage cheese over tomatoes. Top with 1 Tbsp of fresh, chopped chives, 1 slice of hard-cooked egg, and 1 Tbsp of chopped green onions. Season with salt & pepper.

Chicken & Cheese

Lightly butter a slice of white bread and cover with a leaf of Boston lettuce. Top with 2 thin slices of cooked chicken and 1 thin slice of Swiss cheese. Garnish with minced chives and thinly sliced cucumber.

Cottage Cheese & Avocado

Combine 1/3 cup creamed cottage cheese with 2 Tbsp chopped green onions, 1/4 tsp celery salt and salt & pepper to taste. Spread mayonnaise on a slice of pumpernickel and spoon over cottage cheese. Lay thinly sliced avocado over top and sprinkle with seasoning salt.

Hamburger and The Single Parent

For singles who are working parents, it's important to know "how to hamburger" as well as "how to parent." Ground round spans the generation gap and beefs up a variety of quick meals.

Ranch House Beans

Saute 1/2 onion in 1 Tbsp margarine until golden. Add 1/2 lb ground round and cook until meat is brown and crumbly. Drain off fat. Add a 15-oz can of ranch style beans (drained), 1/3 cup grated Cheddar cheese, a pinch of oregano and salt & pepper to taste. Simmer until hot, and cheese is melted. Serves 2.

The Spinach Connection

An easy way to slip Junior the mean green! Brown 1/2 lb ground round until brown and crumbly. Drain off fat. Cook 1/2 of a 10-oz package of frozen chopped spinach according to directions on package. Press out excess liquid, and add spinach to meat in skillet with 2 Tbsp chopped green onions, 1/4 tsp basil, 1/4 tsp oregano, 1/2 tsp salt and 1/4 tsp pepper. Beat together 2 large eggs and gently stir eggs into meat-spinach mixture, cooking over low heat. Before serving, sprinkle over a topping of Parmesan or Cheddar cheese. Serves 2.

Son of Hamburger Helper

Cook 1 1/2 cups macaroni according to package directions. Drain macaroni and spoon into the bottom of a buttered casserole. Melt 1 Tbsp margarine in skillet, saute 1/4 cup onions until tender; add 1/2 lb ground round and cook until meat is brown and crumbly. Season with 1/2 tsp salt. Drain off fat from skillet. Add 2 cups canned tomatoes, 1/2 tsp basil and salt & pepper to taste. Simmer 10 minutes. Pour meat-tomato mixture over macaroni and sprinkle with 1/2 cup Cheddar cheese. Bake until ingredients are hot and cheese melts. Serves 2 to 3.

Tamale Pie

Saute 1/2 of a chopped onion in 1 Tbsp margarine until golden. Add 1/2 lb ground round and cook until meat is brown and crumbly. Season with 1/2 tsp salt and 1/4 tsp pepper. Drain fat from skillet. Add 2 cups canned tomatoes, 1 cup canned Mexicorn, 2 Tbsp sliced black olives, and season with 1/2 tsp chili powder, 1/4 tsp basil, 1/4 tsp oregano and salt & pepper to taste. Simmer 10 minutes. Transfer contents to casserole. Prepare a 8-oz package of corn muffin mix according to directions. Spoon batter over top of Tamale Pie and bake in a 425 degree oven until crust is golden brown. Serves 3.

We're Only Roommates, Mother

The man and woman who live together to share expenses will never win the Good Housekeeping Seal of Approval, but it's an economical lifestyle. Occasionally this arrangement includes a little cooking on the side, or kitchen privileges. Here are a couple of quick snacks to share with your roommate, chum or gentleman boarder.

Huevos con Chile Y Queso

Remove seeds from a 4-oz can of whole green chiles. Stuff each chile with a slice of Jack cheese. Saute chiles in 2 Tbsp melted margarine until cheese melts. Lightly beat together 3 eggs, 1/4 cup half-and-half, and salt & pepper to taste. Pour over chiles and cook over low heat, gently stirring eggs until they are cooked but still moist, like scrambled eggs. Serve with sliced avocado and hot tortillas. Serves 2.

Montezuma Super Snack

As a filling for each flour tortilla, mix together 1/3 cup grated Cheddar cheese, 1 Tbsp diced canned green chiles, 1 slice tomato, cut in half, 1 Tbsp chopped onion, 2 Tbsp Mexican green chile sauce and 2 Tbsp sour cream. Spoon mixture down the center of flour tortilla and fold in half. Melt 3 Tbsp margarine in skillet and saute tortillas on both sides until brown and crispy. If necessary, add more margarine to skillet for each tortilla you cook.

Shanghai Chicken Stir-Fry

The most challenging art of the single cook is the romantic little dinner for two. It has to be spell-binding, mesmerizing—and digestible. We give you a trio of star-crossed dinners, beginning with this northern Chinese stir-fry.

1 whole chicken breast, boned & skinned
1 egg white
4 Tbsp peanut oil
1/2 cup bamboo shoots, diced
1 long, fresh green chile, seeded & diced
1/2 cups peanuts, coarsely chopped
2 tsp cornstarch
1 clove garlic, minced
1 tsp sugar
4 Tbsp soy sauce
3 Tbsp dry sherry
2 tsp fresh ginger, chopped
4 Tbsp green onions, chopped

Cut chicken into slivers. Combine egg white and chicken, stirring to coat chicken. Heat oil in wok or skillet, and add chicken, bamboo shoots and chile. Stir-fry 3 minutes. Add peanuts and stir-fry another 2 minutes. Mix cornstarch, garlic, sugar, soy sauce, sherry and ginger; and stir into wok or skillet. Add onions and mix thoroughly. Heat 1 minute longer. Serve with steamed rice. Serves 2 generously.

Roman Scampi

Light the candles, pour the chilled white wine, and spoon out this tantalizing shrimp flavored with wine and mushrooms. He'll think you've been reading The Total Woman.

8 large scampi shrimp
Salt & pepper to taste
1/3 cup cornflakes, crushed
1/3 cup flour
1/3 cup cracker crumbs
4 Tbsp Parmesan cheese
2 eggs beaten
4 Tbsp olive oil
1 clove garlic
3 green onions, sliced
2 Tbsp parsley, chopped
1 cup mushrooms, sliced
1/4 cup white wine

Peel shrimp and devein. With a knife split the underside of the shrimp lengthwise but do not cut all the way through. Spread apart and flatten or "butterfly" the almost divided halves of shrimp. Sprinkle with salt & pepper to taste. Combine cornflakes, flour, cracker crumbs and cheese. Dip shrimp first in the eggs, then coat with crumb-cheese mixture. Heat oil in skillet, add garlic and cook to golden brown; discard garlic. Add shrimp and cook over medium heat for a few minutes on each side. Remove from skillet. Add green onions, parsley and mushrooms and saute until tender. Put shrimp back into skillet, add wine and simmer several minutes longer. Serve with the following Bean Sprout Salad. Serves 2.

Bean Sprout Salad

To nail down your image as a total woman and total cook, an exquisite little oriental salad.

1/4 lb fresh bean sprouts, washed and dried
1/3 cup celery, finely chopped
4 Tbsp green onions, finely chopped
1/3 cup mayonnaise
1 Tbsp soy sauce
1 tsp curry powder
1 tsp lemon juice

Combine bean sprouts, celery and green onions, Mix together mayonnaise, soy sauce, curry powder and lemon juice. Toss salad with dressing just before serving. Serves 2.

Meatballs for Lovers

*These aren't everyday married meatballs. They're Imperial Russian meatballs —
once relished by Grand Dukes and beautiful ballerinas.*

1/2 lb ground round
1 egg, lightly beaten
1/4 cup bread crumbs
4 Tbsp milk
1/4 tsp nutmeg
1/2 tsp salt
1/4 tsp pepper
2 Tbsp paprika
3 Tbsp margarine
1 cup mushrooms, thinly sliced
1/4 cup green onions, finely chopped
1/4 cup dry sherry
2 Tbsp canned beef gravy
1/3 cup heavy cream
1/2 cup sour cream
2 Tbsp parsley, finely chopped

Mix together ground round and egg. Soak breadcrumbs in milk and add to meat mixture. Season with nutmeg, salt & pepper. Shape meat into meatballs about 1-inch in diameter. Roll meatballs in paprika until well coated. Heat margarine and saute meatballs until lightly browned in about 5 minutes. Gently spoon mushrooms and onions around the meatballs and continue simmering and stirring another 5 minutes. Add sherry, beef gravy and heavy cream. Simmer over low heat another 15 minutes, stirring frequently. Before serving, stir in sour cream and heat, but do not boil. Garnish with parsley. Serve with buttered noodles and the following Glazed Carrots & Onions. Serves 2.

Glazed Carrots & Onions

Carrots with charisma! The secret is the sweet-sharp glaze.

2 small carrots, peeled
6 small white boiling onions
2 cups water
1/2 tsp salt
3 Tbsp margarine
3 Tbsp apricot preserves
3 Tbsp lemon juice
1 Tbsp parsley, chopped

Cut carrots diagonally into 1/2 inch thick slices. Peel onions and cut a small cross in the root end to keep onions whole and firm during cooking. Bring water to a boil, add carrots, onions and salt. Simmer for 10 minutes or until vegetables are tender. Drain. In a skillet, heat margarine, apricot preserves and lemon juice. Add vegetables and gently stir until they're glazed. Garnish with parsley before serving. Serves 2.

Six Friend Casserole

The care and feeding of friends is easiest with a buffet lunch or dinner built around a casserole. This gorgeous concoction is not only a friend-pleaser, but a hostess-saver. Make it the night before.

4 slices white bread
margarine
2 cups Cheddar cheese, shredded
3 cups cooked chicken,
    boned and skinned
2 cups Jack cheese, shredded
4-oz can green chiles, diced & drained
6 eggs, beaten
2 cups milk
2 tsp salt
2 tsp paprika
1 tsp oregano
1 garlic, crushed
1 tsp dry mustard

Trim crusts from bread. Spread one side of each slice with margarine. Place bread, margarine side down, in a greased rectangular baking pan approximately 7 1/2 x 11 1/2. Sprinkle Cheddar cheese evenly over bread. Spoon chicken, cut in bite-size pieces, over cheese. Sprinkle Jack cheese over chicken. Spoon green chiles evenly over top. In a bowl, combine eggs, milk, salt, paprika, oregano, garlic and mustard. Beat well and pour over casserole. Cover, and refrigerate overnight. When ready to serve, bring casserole to room temperature; bake uncovered in a 325 degree oven until top is puffy and lightly browned, about 40 minutes. Serves 6.

Spinach & Lettuce Bowl

To complement your casserole, a toss-up of spinach and lettuce embellished with bacon, onions and croutons. The real dazzler is the dressing.

4 cups spinach
4 cups Boston lettuce
4 slices bacon, diced
2 large eggs
2/3 cup cider vinegar
2/3 cup water
1/4 cup sugar

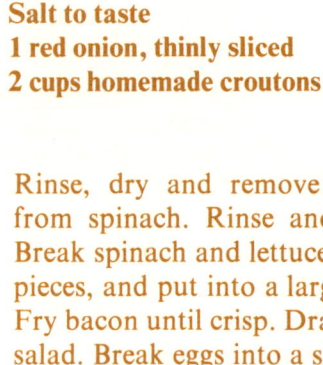

Salt to taste
1 red onion, thinly sliced
2 cups homemade croutons

Rinse, dry and remove tough stems from spinach. Rinse and dry lettuce. Break spinach and lettuce into bite-size pieces, and put into a large salad bowl. Fry bacon until crisp. Drain and add to salad. Break eggs into a sieve set over a bowl. Pour vinegar and water over eggs, forcing mixture through the sieve. Stir sugar into mixture, adding more sugar if a sweeter taste is desired. Pour dressing into a skillet and simmer over low heat, stirring constantly until dressing is creamy and thickened. Season with salt to taste. Pour warm dressing over greens just before serving. Add onion and croutons and toss lightly. Serves 6.

Apricot Alchemy

When you mix corn muffin mix with brown sugar and butter, and bake it with apricots you get ambrosia for dessert. Honest.

1 lb 13-oz can apricot halves
3 Tbsp brown sugar
1/2 stick of butter
1/2 cup brown sugar
1 cup corn muffin mix
Vanilla ice cream

Drain can of apricots and arrange fruit in a shallow, greased baking dish. Sprinkle apricots with brown sugar. Cream together butter with 1/2 cup brown sugar and corn muffin mix. Sprinkle crumbly mixture evenly over fruit. Bake in a 350 degree oven for 40 minutes or until brown and puffy. Serve warm over a good quality vanilla ice cream. Serves 6.

Honey Curried Chicken 74

Another make-ahead party dish that comes on nice and easy with a minimum of trauma from the kitchen.

**2 frying chickens, cut in serving pieces
2 cloves garlic, crushed
Juice of 1 lemon
Salt & pepper to taste
1/2 cup margarine
1 cup honey
2 Tbsp curry powder
2 Tbsp Dijon prepared mustard
1 tsp soy sauce
6 green onions, finely chopped**

Remove skin from chicken. Rub chicken with garlic and season with lemon juice and salt and pepper to taste. Melt margarine and honey in a saucepan and stir in curry powder, mustard and soy sauce and green onions. Place chicken in a single layer in a shallow baking pan and spoon sauce and onions over chicken. Cover with foil and refrigerate for at least four hours, turning the chicken several times. Bake chicken in a 350 degree oven, basting frequently until fowl is tender, in about an hour. Chicken may be cooked ahead of time and re-heated just before serving. Serves 6.

Party Greenery

*Sharing the menu is a nifty salad with fresh green beans,
steamed until they're barely tender.
Please don't cook the crunch out of them.*

2 tomatoes, peeled & quartered
2 cups green beans, steamed
2 heads Boston lettuce
4 hard-cooked eggs, chopped
3/4 cup mayonnaise
1/3 cup sour cream
1 Tbsp lemon juice

1/2 tsp salt (or more to taste)
1/4 tsp paprika
1/4 cup parsley, minced
1 Tbsp onion, grated
1 Tbsp chives or green onions, chopped
1/4 tsp curry
1/2 tsp Worcestershire sauce

In a large salad bowl combine tomatoes, green beans, lettuce (cut in bite-size pieces) and eggs. Prepare a dressing of mayonnaise, sour cream, lemon juice, salt, paprika, parsley, onion, chives or green onions, curry powder and Worcestershire sauce. Spoon dressing into salad just before serving. Serves 6.

Plums in Port Sauce

And for dessert, rich, poetic plums wrapped in a spicy port wine sauce.

2 lbs plums
Grated peel of 1/2 orange
6 whole cloves
1 stick cinnamon, 3 to 4 inches long
2 cups port wine
1 cup sugar

Slash each plum to the pit on one side. In a large, heavy saucepan combine plums, orange peel, cloves, cinnamon, wine and sugar. Bring to boil and simmer, uncovered, about 10 minutes or until plums begin to soften. (Cooking time varies with the size and ripeness of fruit.) Cool plums. Transfer from saucepan to a container and pour port sauce over fruit. Cover, and refrigerate for one or two days. Serve with syrup. Makes 6 servings.

Chapter V

The Gourmet Dude

For the gourmet dude whose hobby is plying beautiful women with exquisite food and drink, we offer a tantalizing collection of epicurean delights. Also on the menu are cloud nine breakfasts for two. Unlike the married breakfast, this romantic repast bans hair curlers and newspapers.

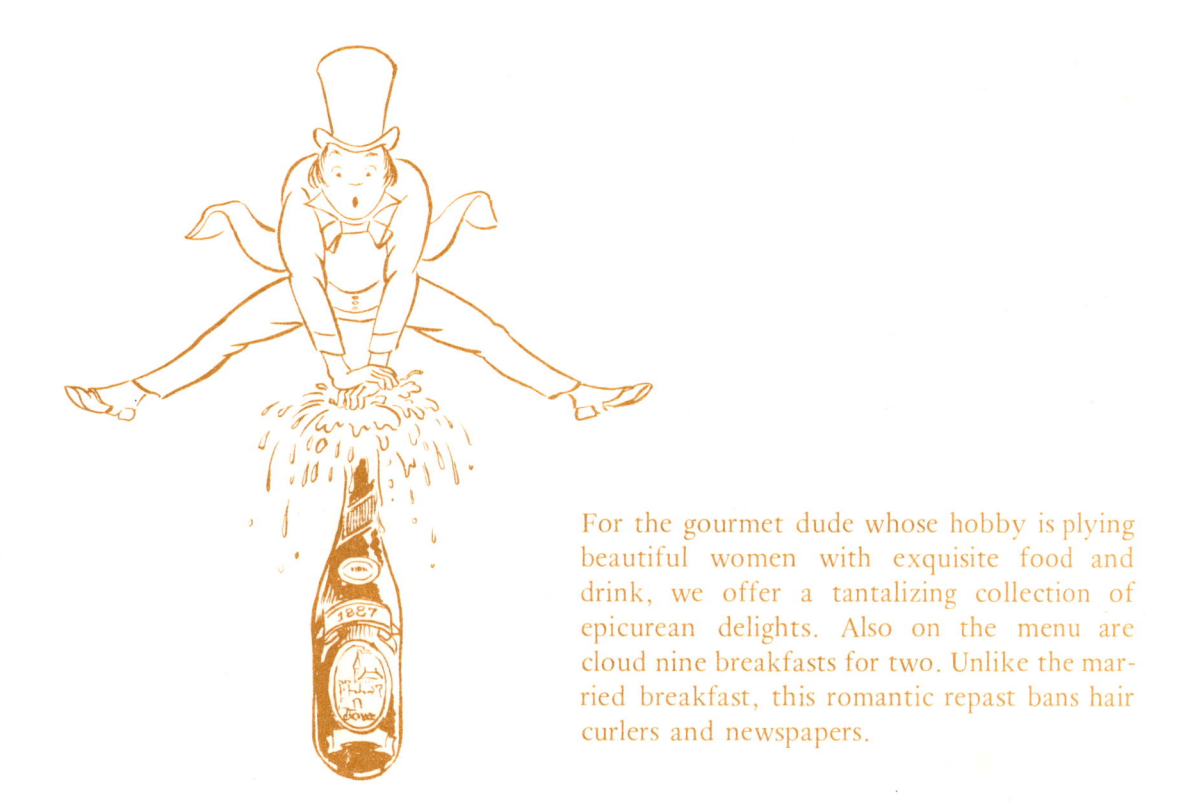

Gigot Provencale

*One of the arts of wolf-craft is the ability to roast a Gigot,
or French leg of lamb, to pink perfection.
If you plan to be distracted before dinner, better set the timer.*

1 clove of garlic, slivered
3 1/2 to 4-lb leg of lamb
1/2 tsp thyme
1/2 tsp tarragon
1 tsp salt

1/2 tsp corasely ground pepper
1 tsp rosemary
1/3 cup olive oil
2 Tbsp lemon juice

Insert slivers of garlic into lamb in several places. Rub lamb with a mixture of thyme, tarragon, and salt & pepper. In a saucepan combine rosemary with olive oil and lemon juice. Heat for 3 minutes. Place lamb, skin side up, on rack over shallow pan. Brush with seasoned olive oil. Roast meat in a preheated 450 degree oven for 15 minutes to seal in juices, then reduce temperature to 350. Meat should be roasted 12 to 15 minutes per lb for medium rare or pink lamb. (If you prefer lamb that is less pink, increase cooking time.) Baste meat frequently with seasoned olive oil.

Bachelor Breasts

These breasts will never make the centerfold of Playboy Magazine, but they're worth adding to your collection.

4 chicken breast halves
Salt & pepper to taste
4 Tbsp margarine
1 cup mushrooms, sliced
1/4 cup dry sherry
8 thin slices Mozzarella cheese

Bone breasts and remove skin. Put breasts between pieces of waxed paper and flatten them with a mallet or knife handle. Season with salt & pepper to taste. Heat margarine in a skillet and saute breasts over low heat until golden brown and tender. Remove chicken from skillet. Add mushrooms and saute until tender. Pour in sherry and simmer another minute. Place breasts in a shallow baking dish. Spoon over mushrooms, and the juices from the skillet. Top each breast with 2 thin slices of Mozzarella cheese. Run baking dish under broiler; heat until cheese melts a little. Serves 2.

Steak Satay

*An intriguing skewered beef from Indonesia.
Perfect for your James Bond image.*

1 lb top sirloin
1/4 cup butter
1/3 cup soy sauce
2 Tbsp lemon juice
1 Tbsp chili powder
1/4 tsp salt
1/4 tsp pepper

Remove fat from steak and cut into 1-inch cubes. Thread meat on small skewers. (Wooden skewers are usually available in meat markets.) Blend together butter, soy sauce, lemon juice, chili powder and salt & pepper. Brush steak liberally with sauce 1 hour before broiling. Broil over coals, or under broiler, to desired taste, basting frequently. Serves 2. Try this with Barley Bowl on page 28.

Fresh Salmon Francaise

*When there's something beautiful between the two of you,
it could be this exquisite French Salmon.*

2 fresh salmon fillets
1/2 cup fresh, sliced mushrooms
2 green onions, finely chopped
1 tomato, peeled & diced
1/3 cup white wine
1 Tbsp lemon juice

Salt & pepper to taste
3 Tbsp margarine
1 Tbsp flour
1 egg yolk
1/3 cup heavy cream
1 Tbsp parsley, finely chopped

Place salmon in a shallow baking dish, and add mushrooms, onions, tomato, white wine, lemon juice, and season with salt & pepper to taste. Dot fish with 2 Tbsp of the margarine. Cover baking dish with foil, and bake 15 minutes in a 400 degree oven. Remove salmon, place in a serving casserole and keep warm. Pour the remaining vegetables and sauce into a skillet and simmer over low heat for 1 minute. Mix the remaining tablespoon of margarine with flour and stir into skillet with a wire whisk. Remove skillet from stove. Beat egg yolk and cream together, and add a little sauce from the skillet, then stir egg-cream mixture back into skillet. Pour contents over salmon in serving casserole, sprinkle with parsley and run casserole under the broiler for a couple of minutes until sauce is golden brown. Serves 2.

Parisian French Bread

*The gourmet dude makes French bread with a crust
that goes crunch when you bite into it.*

1 package dry yeast
1/2 tsp sugar
1 cup lukewarm water
1/2 tsp salt
2 Tbsp soft margarine
3 1/2 cups sifted white flour

Dissolve yeast and sugar in lukewarm water. Add salt and butter. Stir in 2 cups sifted flour into yeast mixture. Gradually work in 1 1/2 cups more of the sifted flour. Knead dough on floured surface until smooth. Cover and let rise until doubled in size. Punch down dough, cover and let rise 30 minutes. Divide dough in half and shape into 2 long rolls 1 1/2 inches in diameter. Place on greased baking sheet and let rise until doubled in size. Brush with water; make diagonal slashes on top. Place a shallow pan of hot water in the bottom of oven. Bake loaves in preheated 400 degree oven for 45 minutes until crusty brown. Makes 2 loaves.

Tomato & Mozzarella Salad

Every bachelor needs a couple of great salads in his act.

Select 2 of the most beautiful, flavorful tomatoes you can find — preferably Beefsteak Tomatoes. Peel and thinly slice the tomatoes. Thinly slice 6 or more pieces of Mozzarella cheese the same size as the tomato slices. Alternate slices of tomato and cheese on a salad plate. Spoon over your favorite French dressing and garnish with chopped parsley. Serves 2.

Open Sesame Salad

Rinse and dry 1 small head of Boston lettuce, broken into bite-size pieces. In a salad bowl, combine lettuce with 1/4 cup thinly sliced water chestnuts, 2 Tbsp toasted sesame seeds and 1/4 cup grated Parmesan cheese. Toss salad just before serving with any salad dressing of your choice. Serves 2.

Korean Beef Barbecue

Another exotic barbecue to demonstrate your well-traveled tastes. The Korean name for this is Bul Gogi. No bul.

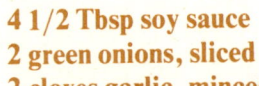

4 1/2 Tbsp soy sauce
2 green onions, sliced
2 cloves garlic, minced
1 Tbsp sesame oil
2 Tbsp sugar
1/4 tsp pepper
1 thin slice fresh ginger, minced
1 Tbsp toasted sesame seeds
1 lb top sirloin

Combine soy sauce, onions, garlic, sesame oil, sugar, pepper, ginger and sesame seeds in a bowl. Cut all fat from steak. With a sharp knife, cut the meat across the grain slightly on an angle into 1/4-inch slices. Cut each slice into halves to make uniform strips. Add meat to marinade, and marinate for a couple of hours. Broil meat to rare, medium or well done, as desired. Serves 2.

Veiled Chicken

*This sensuous, middle eastern chicken is seductive bait for innocent prey —
if you can find any innocent prey.*

4 chicken breast halves, boned & skinned
4 Tbsp margarine
Salt to taste
4 Tbsp honey
4 Tbsp margarine
1 Tbsp lemon juice
2 Tbsp sesame seeds, toasted
1 Tbsp parsley, chopped

Saute breasts in margarine until tender and lightly browned. Salt to taste. Place breasts in shallow pan. In a skillet combine honey, margarine, lemon juice, sesame seeds and parsley. Heat until honey and margarine melts. Spoon sauce over breasts. Bake in a preheated 350 degree oven for 5 minutes. Serves 2.

Tempura Without Tears

*We've broken the Japanese code.
The secret of perfect shrimp tempura is chilled batter and hot oil —
so put on your Happi coat and start frying.*

3 cups cake flour
2 eggs, beaten
2 cups ice water
8 large shrimp
oil for deep frying
All-purpose flour
Butter
3 large mushrooms, sliced
1 sweet potato,
     peeled & cut into strips
6 whole green beans

Mix cake flour, eggs and ice water until batter is lumpy. Chill in fridge. Shell shrimp leaving tails intact. Flatten the shrimp slightly with the flat side of a heavy knife so they won't curl in frying. Heat oil in electric skillet to 350 degrees. (Make sure oil remains the same temperature during cooking). Remove chilled batter from fridge and beat briefly. Dip shrimp into all-purpose flour and then into chilled batter. Shake off excess batter and drop shrimp into hot fat. When shrimp rises to surface, dab a bit of butter on each shrimp and continue frying until batter is puffy, golden brown and crisp. Turn once and remove shrimp with a slotted spoon. Drain on wire rack. Keep shrimp warm while you cook vegetables. Dip mushrooms, sweet potato strips and green beans first into all-purpose flour and then into chilled batter; and fry the same as the shrimp — until golden brown and crisp. Serve with the following Tempura Sauce.

Combine 1/2 cup soy with 1/4 cup sake or rice wine, 1/2 cup water and 1 tsp Accent. Bring to a simmer and pour into individual dipping bowls. Spoon in a dab of grated white radish into each bowl. Serves 2.

Bruce Zimmerman's Bananas Flambe

Here's a dessert from a bachelor friend who performs this flaming spectacular without a fire permit.

**2 Tbsp butter
2 Tbsp brown sugar
1/2 tsp vanilla
1/4 tsp cinnamon
1/4 cup *fresh* orange juice
Juice of 1/2 lemon
3 bananas, cut in halves
1/4 cup Banana liqueur
Grated rind of 1/2 orange & 1/2 lemon**

Melt butter in skillet. Add sugar and stir until melted. Stir in vanilla, cinnamon, orange juice and lemon juice. Add sliced bananas to skillet and cook only 1 minute on each side to heat through; do not overcook or they'll turn mushy. Remove bananas from skillet. Heat orange-lemon sauce in skillet for another minute. In a separate saucepan, warm Banana liqueur and poor into skillet. Ignite sauce with a match and continue to stir. Simmer until sauce cooks down and thickens enough to coat the back of a spoon. Arrange bananas on top of French vanilla ice cream, and pour over sauce. Garnish with grated orange and lemon rind. Serves 2.

Spiked Peaches

Another spirited dessert to warm a lady's heart.

1/4 cup butter
2 small fresh peaches, peeled & halved
1 Tbsp grated orange peel
1 tsp lemon juice
2 Tbsp brown sugar
2 oz bourbon, warmed
Garnish: toasted almonds, finely chopped

Melt butter and saute peaches until lightly browned. Add orange peel, lemon juice and sugar. Cook until sugar melts. Pour in warmed bourbon and ignite with a match. Place peaches on top of French vanilla ice cream and spoon over sauce. Garnish with toasted almonds. Serves 2.

The Late, Late Show

*Keep a well-stocked fridge for middle of the night emergencies.
Like the petite blonde with the gargantuan appetite.
She'll love this sizzling sandwich.*

**4 slices white bread
butter
4 slices Swiss cheese
2 slices cooked chicken**

For each sandwich, butter 2 slices of bread. On one slice of bread put a slice of Swiss cheese, a slice of cooked chicken, and another slice of Swiss cheese. Cover with remaining slice of bread. Press sandwich firmly together. Butter the outside of the sandwich on both sides. Saute sandwich in a lightly greased skillet on both sides until bread is toasted and cheese melts a little. Makes 2 sandwiches.

Swiss Eggs

Any dude worth his seasoning salt stirs up a nifty breakfast for two.
These Swiss Eggs, seasoned with a touch of sherry,
belong in your basic training manual.

2 Tbsp margarine
1/4 cup heavy cream
1/3 cup grated Swiss cheese
4 eggs, beaten
1/2 tsp salt
1 Tbsp margarine
2 Tbsp dry sherry
4 toasted English muffin halves
4 thin slices boiled ham

Melt margarine in top of double boiler. Add cream and heat. Stir in cheese. When cheese is almost melted, gently stir in eggs, which have been seasoned with salt. Stir eggs from the bottom of the pan. When eggs are softly scrambled, add 1 more tablespoon of margarine and sherry. Spoon eggs on toasted, buttered English muffin halves which have been covered with a slice of boiled ham. Serves 2.

Huevos Rancheros

This breakfast for two is quicker to produce if you make the sauce the day before. But first check your horoscope to be sure you're going to make friendly contacts that evening.

2 Tbsp margarine
1/3 cup onions, finely chopped
1/3 cup bell pepper, finely chopped
1/2 clove garlic, minced
1 tsp flour
2 cups canned tomatoes

1 tsp chili powder
1 tsp salt
1/2 tsp pepper
4 eggs
1/2 cup Jack cheese, cubed
Buttered tortillas

Melt margarine and saute onions and bell pepper and garlic until tender. Add flour. Spoon in tomatoes, breaking them into small pieces, and season with chili powder, salt & pepper. Simmer 10 minutes. Spoon tomato sauce equally into 2 shallow, individual baking dishes. Break 2 eggs carefully into each dish on top of the sauce. Place cubes of cheese around and between the eggs. Bake in a 350 degree oven until eggs are firm but still soft in the middle, about 10 minutes. Serve with hot, buttered tortillas. Serves 2.

Orange Toast with Honey Sauce

Whether she's an activist, feminist or Buddhist — all chicks love French toast in the morning.

3 egg yolks, beaten
1/3 cup light cream
1/4 cup *fresh* orange juice
1 tsp grated orange rind
1/8 tsp nutmeg
Dash of salt
4 slices white bread
3 Tbsp margarine
1/3 cup honey
1 Tbsp lemon juice
1 Tbsp margarine

Beat egg yolks with light cream. Add orange juice, orange rind, nutmeg and salt. Dip each bread slice into egg mixture, turning it to coat both sides. Melt margarine in skillet and pan fry bread on both sides until a golden color, but not brown. Keep toast warm. Heat honey, lemon juice and margarine in a separate skillet. Spoon over toast before serving. Serves 2.

Cloud Nine Sangria

Sangria is bachelor brew—light, delicious and heady. Perfect for a cloud nine breakfast.

**1 fifth dry red wine
1/2 cup apple juice
1 1/2 oz brandy
2 Tbsp sugar
1 orange, thinly sliced
1 lemon, thinly sliced
1 cup fresh fruit: whole strawberries or diced peaches**

Mix wine, apple juice, brandy, sugar, orange and lemon slices and fruit in a large pitcher. Press fruit slices against pitcher with a wooden spoon to extract some of the juice. Add a generous amount of ice cubes, stir and serve.

Chapter VI

City Lunches and Country Picnics

The lunchtime trauma of crowded restaurants and high tabs is easily solved with a homemade lunch. Brown bagging is your best revenge against mediocre food and wall-to-wall people. Thanks to thermoses, brown bag lunches carry hot soups, chilled salads — or most anything you like. There's also an interesting assortment of grown-up sandwiches you can pack that don't taste like the ones that mother used to make.

Whether it's a lunch hour picnic in the park, or a country banquet complete with babbling brook — the portable feast is the only way to go.

The Fourth Earl of Sandwich's Noblest Creations

John Montague, Earl of Sandwich, solved the lunchtime crisis with an ingenious invention that travels compactly in brown bag, lunch pail or executive briefcase. Here are some ways to vary your daily bread.

Riviera Sandwich

Split a hero-size roll of French or Italian bread lengthwise, and rub with a clove of garlic. Arrange 2 slices of Jack cheese or Bel Paese cheese along bottom half of roll. Top with 1 thin slice of red onion, 1 slice of tomato, 1 pimiento sliced, and several black, sliced olives. Mix 1/2 Tbsp olive oil, 1/2 Tbsp wine vinegar, 1/4 tsp basil, 1/4 tsp oregano; and spoon over sandwich. Cover with other half of roll.

Cream Cheese & Chicken

Mix 1 Tbsp sour cream and 1 Tbsp cream cheese with 1/2 tsp caraway seeds. Butter 2 slices of white bread. Put a slice of cooked chicken on one slice of bread and spread cream cheese mixture over the top. Season with salt & pepper. Cover with a second slice of chicken and the remaining slice of bread.

Ham, Cucumber & Cheese

Butter 2 slices of pumpernickel bread. Layer bread with 1 slice of ham, several thin slices of cucumbers and 1 slice of Swiss cheese. Cover with remaining slice of bread.

Bagel with Cream Cheese & Lox

Split a bagel and spread cream cheese on both halves. On one half lay 2 thin slices of Lox smoked salmon. Squeeze a little lemon juice on top. Close bagel.

Tuna Fish & Cheese

Drain and flake 1/4 cup tuna fish, and combine with 2 Tbsp diced Swiss cheese, 1 Tbsp bell pepper and sufficient mayonnaise to blend ingredients. Season with a sprinkling of onion salt, dill weed and 1/2 tsp lemon juice. Butter 2 slices of whole grain bread, and spread filling between.

Heroine Sandwich

Split a French or Italian hero-size roll lengthwise, and brush each side with Italian dressing. On bottom half of roll, arrange a couple of slices of Italian salami, Mortadella and Provolone cheese. Add a slice of tomato and a few Italian peppers. Cover with the other half of the roll.

Avocado & Cheese

Butter 2 slices of whole grain bread. On one slice arrange a layer of thinly sliced avocado and season with salt and lemon juice. Top with a layer of thinly sliced Cheddar cheese and alfalfa sprouts. Cover with remaining slice of bread.

Green Pepper Sandwich

Remove seeds from a green or red bell pepper. Chop 3 Tbsp of the pepper finely and blend with 2 oz of softened cream cheese. Season with salt & pepper to taste. Butter 2 slices of rye bread and spread filling between.

Tomato & Basil

Mix 1/2 tsp basil with 2 Tbsp butter. Spread herb butter on 2 slices of white toast. Peel and seed 1 small tomato. Chop finely, salt to taste and spoon tomato between slices of toast.

Triple-Deck Salmon Sandwich

Combine 1/4 cup canned salmon, drained & flaked, 1 Tbsp chopped green onion, 1 Tbsp chopped celery, 1 Tbsp lemon juice, a sprinkling of dill weed and sufficient mayonnaise to blend ingredients. Spread mayonnaise on 3 slices of wheat bread. On bottom slice, spoon over salmon mixture. Cover with second slice of bread, and layer thinly sliced cucumbers. Season with salt. Cover with remaining slice of bread.

Laguna Beach Hero

Split a hero-size roll of Italian or French bread lengthwise. Brush with olive oil. On bottom half, sprinkle a layer of chopped green onions, a layer of tuna fish, a layer of sliced hard-cooked eggs, a layer of thinly sliced tomatoes and a sprinkling of sliced black olives. Season with salt & pepper. Cover with top of roll.

Brown Bag Salads

These non-wilt salads stay cool, calm and collected in a squat wide-mouth thermos. With crackers and cheese on the side, you have a refreshing little feast, especially welcome in the summer. Chill salads before you put them into the thermos.

Cannellini Bean Salad

Combine 1/2 cup canned, drained cannellini beans (rinsed in cold water) with 1/4 cup flaked drained tuna fish, 2 Tbsp green chopped onions, 1 Tbsp chopped parsley, 1/2 tsp basil, 1/2 clove crushed garlic, 2 Tbsp olive oil, 1 Tbsp salad oil, 2 Tbsp wine vinegar and salt & pepper to taste. Mix well. Cannellini beans are sold in Italian food markets and some supermarkets.

Cucumber with Mint & Dill

Peel and thinly slice 1/2 a cucumber. Lightly salt cucumber and mix with 1/4 cup yogurt, 1/2 tsp dill weed and 1 tsp fresh or dried mint.

Green Bean Salad

Combine 1 cup canned French-cut green beans (drained) with 1 Tbsp diced pimiento, and 2 Tbsp green onions. Mix together 1/4 cup sour cream with 1 Tbsp vinegar, 1/2 tsp Dijon prepared mustard, 1/2 tsp salt and 1/4 tsp pepper. Spoon over beans and mix lightly.

Tuna Salad

Combine 1/2 cup of flaked, drained tuna fish with 2 Tbsp chopped green onions, and 1 hard-cooked chopped egg. Toss salad with 1/4 cup mayonnaise which has been seasoned with 1 Tbsp lemon juice, 1/2 tsp dill week and 1/4 tsp salt.

Egg & Celery Salad

Blanch 1/2 cup thinly sliced celery in boiling water for 1 minute. Mix 1/4 cup mayonnaise with 1 tsp white wine vinegar and 1 Tbsp Dijon prepared mustard. Chop 1 hard-cooked egg and combine with celery. Lightly toss with seasoned mayonnaise and sprinkle with 1 tsp chopped parsley.

Russian Salad

Combine 1/4 cup cooked, diced green beans, 1/4 cup cooked diced carrots, 1/4 cup cooked diced potatoes, 4 Tbsp cooked diced celery and 1 chopped hard-cooked egg. Toss vegetables with 1/3 cup mayonnaise seasoned with salt & pepper.

Pocket Picnics

Pocket picnics are nourishing nibbles for any time, any place. They're small enough to tuck into a ski jacket and light enough to soar in a hang glider.

Stuffed Eggs with Tuna Fish

Cut 4 hard-cooked eggs in half lengthwise and remove yolks. Mash yolks and blend with 3 Tbsp flaked, drained tuna fish, 1 tsp Parmesan cheese, 1 Tbsp butter, 3 Tbsp mayonnaise, 1/2 tsp Worcestershire sauce, 1 tsp minced chives, 1 tsp minced parsley, a dash of Tabasco and salt & pepper to taste. Spoon into egg white cavities, and wrap well in foil. Serves 4.

Chinese Meatballs

The perfect snack to take to your Kung Fu lesson.

Combine 1/2 lb ground round with 4 finely chopped water chestnuts, 2 Tbsp minced green onions, 1 Tbsp soy sauce, 1 beaten egg yolk, 1/2 tsp salt and 1/4 cup breadcrumbs. Shape into small balls about 1-inch in diameter. Bake in a 400 degree oven until meatballs are cooked and lightly browned, about 20 minutes. Serves 4.

Stuffed Ham Rolls

When it's Saturday night at the movies, these hot ham rolls will give you stamina to endure shark bites, earthquakes, holocausts and rape.

Combine 1/2 cup finely chopped ham with 1 hard-cooked chopped egg, 1/4 cup shredded Cheddar cheese, 2 Tbsp celery, 1/2 tsp chopped sweet pickle, 2 tsp brown mustard and enough mayonnaise to blend ingredients. Split 2 hard rolls and remove most of the inside bread. Butter bread cavity. Fill halves with ham mixture and replace top. Cover roll with foil and heat in oven until hot and crispy. Serves 2.

Antipasto

This is the world's first fold 'n carry appetizer.

Remove outside casing from 6 slices of Mortadella salami. Blend 6 heaping Tbsp of tuna fish with 4 Tbsp mayonnaise. On each slice of salami, spoon 1 heaping Tbsp of tuna fish and sprinkle with 1 Tbsp chopped hard-cooked egg. Place a chunk of Bel Paese cheese or Jack cheese on top. Roll up salami and fasten with a toothpick. Serves 2.

Piroshki

For the spy that came in from the cold — or the skier — intriguing little Russian turnovers that self-destruct in one mouthful.

Saute 1/2 finely chopped onion in 1 Tbsp margarine until tender. Add 1/2 lb ground round and cook until brown and crumbly. Drain off fat. Season with 1/2 tsp salt and 1/4 tsp pepper. Remove from heat and combine meat mixture with 1 finely chopped hard-cooked egg, 1/4 cup cooked rice, 1/3 cup sour cream and mix well. Prepare pie crust mix; roll out dough 1/8-inch thick and cut into 3-inch circles. Spoon 1 heaping Tbsp of filling on each round; moisten edges of dough and fold over, sealing edges with fork. Bake in a preheated 350 degree oven for 25 minutes or until brown. Serves 4.

Gazpacho, Anyone?

Take a soup picnic to the tennis court — a thermos of icy cold Gazpacho soup to keep your cool.

2 hard-cooked egg yolks
2 Tbsp olive oil
1 clove crushed garlic
2 tsp Worcestershire sauce
1 tsp dry mustard
Dash of Tabasco sauce
Juice of 1/2 lemon
1 qt tomato juice
Salt & pepper to taste
1/3 cup finely chopped cucumber
1/3 cup finely chopped red onion
1/2 green Bell pepper,
 seeded & finely chopped
2 hard-cooked egg whites, diced
3 strips pimiento, chopped

Mash egg yolks with olive oil to make a paste. Stir in garlic, Worcestershire sauce, mustard, Tabasco and lemon juice. Blend with tomato juice and season with salt & pepper to taste. Stir in cucumber, red onion, green pepper, egg whites and pimiento. Chill soup in fridge at least 3 hours before pouring into thermos. Serves 4.

Quick Clam Chowder 106

*When you're sailing over the bounding main,
a warming mug of clam chowder revives drenched spirits.*

3 white onions, chopped
6 slices lean bacon, diced
4 potatoes, peeled & diced
**2 7 1/2-oz cans minced clams
     with liquid**
1 1/2 qts milk
1 Tbsp Worcestershire sauce
Salt & pepper to taste
2 Tbsp margarine

Fry onions and bacon together until both begin to brown. Add potatoes, clams, and milk. Season with Worcestershire sauce, salt & pepper to taste and margarine. Simmer slowly until potatoes are cooked. Serves 4 to 6.

Basque Barbecued Lamb

Some picnics are full blown banquets unfolding in wooden glen
or sylvan vale where forest nymphs and satyrs dwell —
as well as that stalwart ranger and house detective, Smokey the Bear.
Nothing could celebrate a beautiful day more tastily
than this basque lamb grilled on your portable barbecue.

1/2 cup olive oil
1/2 cup white vinegar
1/2 cup dry white wine
1 clove garlic, minced

1/2 tsp sage
1 tsp salt
1 tsp pepper
6 round-bone lamb chops

Combine olive oil, vinegar, white wine, garlic, sage, salt and pepper. Pour marinade over lamb chops turning meat so it is well coated. Marinate lamb in fridge for 24 hours. Wrap chops in foil and transport in ice chest along with marinade. Grill chops 8 to 10 minutes on each side, basting frequently with marinade. If you're feeling affluent, a butterflied leg of lamb may be used instead of the chops. Serves 6.

Basque Picnic Beans

The other half of a basque picnic are these mellow beans that are kept hot in a thermal container — or a casserole double-wrapped in heavy foil and then in newspapers.

1 lb pink beans
1 Tbsp salt
1/2 tsp pepper
1/2 lb ground round
1 onion, chopped
2 tsp chili powder
1/2 tsp garlic powder
1 large ham hock

Cover beans with water. Bring to a boil. Remove from heat and let beans soak 1 hour. Add more water to cover, season with salt & pepper and simmer beans 1 hour. Brown ground round in skillet, add onion and saute until onions are tender. Drain fat. Add meat and onions to beans; season with chili powder and garlic powder. Add ham hock, cover and simmer until beans are tender. Remove ham hock, cut meat from bone and discard bone. Cube ham and return meat to pot. Serves 6.

San Blas Surfer Steaks

*Beach banquet, Mexican style.
The Guacamole sauce is hot enough to burn a hole in your wet suit,
so keep enough beer to extinquish the fire.
For a milder sauce, reduce the amount of chiles.*

6 steaks, any variety
1 1/2 tsp thyme
1 1/2 tsp salt
Juice of 1/2 lemon
Lemon peel
1/3 cup onions, finely chopped
Melted butter
3 small white boiling onions,
**   peeled & minced**
1 Tbsp cilantro parsley, chopped
2 small hot chiles, chopped
6 small, very ripe tomatoes,
**   peeled & chopped**
2 cloves garlic, crushed
1/2 tsp ground oregano
Salt & pepper to taste
Juice of 1 lemon
1 very ripe avocado, peeled

Sprinkle steaks on both sides with thyme, salt and lemon juice. Rub steaks with lemon peel and pat chopped onions onto meat. Grill steaks over hot coals, basting with melted butter until meat is cooked to individual tastes. Serve with the following Guacamole Sauce:

In a bowl mash together onions, cilantro, chiles, tomatoes, garlic, oregano, salt & pepper to taste and lemon juice. Mash avocado and gradually add to sauce. This sauce is also super with broiled hamburgers.

Grilled Corn on the Cob

The best corn on — or off — the cob. Serve with Surfer Steaks.

6 ears of young, sweet corn
Butter
Seasoning salt to taste
1 cup grated Cheddar cheese

Remove husks and silk from ears of corn. Spread corn lavishly with butter and seasoning salt, and sprinkle with Cheddar cheese. Double wrap corn in foil. Broil 6 to 8 inches from coals, turning ears every 3 to 4 minutes until corn is roasted and cheese melts, about 10 minutes. Serves 6.

Cool Chicken

What do you take to a rock concert that's legal?
What else, man, but a picnic basket of fried chicken and potato salad?

2 small fryers, cut in serving pieces
1 1/2 cups cooking oil
2 eggs, beaten
1 tsp oregano
1 tsp rosemary
1 tsp tarragon
1 tsp paprika
2 cloves garlic, crushed
2 cups flour
2 tsp salt
1 tsp pepper
4 cups cooking oil
Salt to taste

Rinse and dry chicken pieces, and place in a shallow pan. Combine oil, eggs, oregano, rosemary, tarragon, paprika & garlic, and pour marinade over chicken. Turn chicken in marinade to coat both sides. Let chicken marinate 2 hours or more. Remove from pan and dip chicken in flour seasoned with salt & pepper. Pour 2 cups of cooking oil in each of two skillets. Heat oil until it is hot enough to sizzle when tested with a drop of water. Brown chicken pieces quickly on all sides. Cover pans, reduce heat and cook chicken slowly until tender, about 30 minutes or more. Season chicken during cooking with additional salt to taste. Drain chicken on paper towels before wrapping for picnic. Serves 6.

Underground Potato Salad

This potato salad will never make it with the Daughters of the American Revolution. There weren't any bean sprouts at Concord.

4 large red boiling potatoes, peeled
3/4 cup bean sprouts, rinsed
1/4 cup green onions, finely chopped
Salt & pepper to taste
Lemon Dill Dressing:
    1/2 cup salad oil
    1/4 cup lemon juice
    1 tsp dill weed
    1/2 tsp dry mustard
    1/2 tsp salt
    1/2 tsp sugar

Cut potatoes into 1/4-inch slices and steam until tender. Combine potatoes with bean sprouts, green onions and season with salt & pepper to taste. Mix together the Lemon Dill Dressing: salad oil, lemon juice, dill weed, dry mustard, salt and sugar. Spoon dressing over potato salad before serving. Serves 6.

Genesis Apple Cake

It was an apple that turned friends into lovers.
God only knows what this apple cake will do for you.

2 cups sugar
1 1/2 cups vegetable oil
2 tsp vanilla
2 eggs, beaten
Juice of 1/2 lemon, strained
1 tsp salt
3 cups white flour
1 1/2 tsp baking soda
3 cups apples, peeled & chopped
1 1/2 cups pecans, broken

Mix together sugar, vegetable oil, vanilla, eggs, lemon juice and salt. Sift together flour and soda, and stir into sugar-egg mixture. Add apples, and pecans (which have been lightly dusted with flour). Pour batter into a buttered angel food cake pan. Bake at 375 degrees for 1 hour or until done. Cool.

Index

Abie's Irish Corned Beef	49
Antipasto	104
Apple, Cheese & Walnut	61
Apricot Alchemy	73
Avocado & Cheese	97
Avocado Stuffed with Salmon Salad	47
Bachelor Breasts	79
Bagel with Cream Cheese & Lox	96
Baked Acorn Squash with Pineapple	36
Baked Eggs Florentine	8
Barley Bowl with Mushrooms	28
Basque Barbecued Lamb	107
Basque Picnic Beans	108
Bean Burrito, Peso-Pinchers	53
Bean & Green Salad	30
Bean Sprout Salad	68

Beef:
Abie's Irish Corned Beef	49
Chinese Meatballs	103
El Hamburger	58
Korean Beef Barbecue	84
Meatballs for Lovers	69
Monday Night Meatball	7
New Mexico Green Chile Chili	46
Piroshki	104
Ranch House Beans	62
San Blas Surfer Steaks	109
Son of Hamburger Helper	63
Steak Satay	80
Sunday Thru Tuesday Pot Roast	20
Tamale Pie	63
The Best Beef Stew	43
The Spinach Connection	62

Breads:
Honey Marmalade Nut Bread	19
Honey Walnut Bread	31
Muffled Carrot Muffins	34
Parisian French Bread	82
Zucchini Bread	51

Broccoli Spectacular	32
Bruce Zimmerman's Bananas Flambe	87
Cannellini Bean Salad	100

Casseroles:
Barley Bowl with Mushrooms	28
Basque Picnic Beans	108
Broccoli Spectacular	32
Chicken, Rice & Sour Cream Casserole	12
French Beans & Lamb Casserole	17

Lazy Lasagne	18
Rice and . . .	50
Six Friend Casserole	71
The Second Time Around	15
Chicken Enchiladas	16
Chicken & Cheese	61
Chicken Soup That Mother Never Made	45
Chicken, Rice & Sour Cream Casserole	12
Chinese Meatballs	103
Cloud Nine Sangria	93
Cool Chicken	111
Cottage Cheese Mix	59
Cottage Cheese & Avocado	61
Cream Cheese & Chicken	95
Cream Cheese Special	60
Cucumber with Mint & Dill	100
Curried Green Beans	33
Curried Lamb	40
Danish Salmon Sandwich	60
Day Before Payday Soy Grit Tacos	14
Desserts:	
Apricot Alchemy	73
Bruce Zimmerman's Bananas Flambe	87
Fresh Lemon Loaf	21
Genesis Apple Cake	113
Plums in Port Sauce	76
Spiked Peaches	88
Diet Chicken	59
Dinner Omelet	44
Dr. Fu Manchu's Chinese Stir-Fry	29
Egg & Celery Salad	101
Eggs:	
Baked Eggs Florentine	8
Dinner Omelet	44
Huevos con Chile y Queso	64
Huevos Rancheros	91
Orange Toast with Honey Sauce	92
Scrambled Eggs and . . .	57
Stuffed Eggs with Tuna Fish	102
Swiss Eggs	88
The Spinach Connection	62
El Hamburger	58
Fowl:	
Bachelor Breasts	79
Chicken Enchiladas	16
Chicken & Cheese Sandwich	61
Chicken, Rice & Sour Cream Casserole	12
Chicken Soup That Mother Never Made	45

Cool Chicken	111	Homemade Fettucine with Mushroom Sauce		9
Cream Cheese & Chicken Sandwich	95	Honey Curried Chicken		74
Diet Chicken	59	Honey Marmalade Nut Bread		19
Honey Curried Chicken	74	Honey Walnut Bread		31
John Wayne Turkey	42	Huevos con chile y Queso		64
Shanghai Chicken Stir-Fry	66	Huevos Rancheros		91
Six Friend Casserole	71			
The Friday Night Bird	54	John Wayne Turkey		42
The Late, Late Show	89			
Veiled Chicken	85	Korean Beef Barbecue		84
Velly Fast Chinese Chicken Salad	52			
French Beans & Lamb Casserole	17	Laguna Beach Hero		99
Fresh Lemon Loaf	21	Lamb:		
Fresh Salmon Francaise	81	Basque Picnic Lamb		107
		Curried Lamb		40
Gazpacho, Anyone?	105	French Beans & Lamb Casserole		17
Genesis Apple Cake	113	Gigot Provencale		78
Gigot Provencale	78	Mediterranean Lamb Shanks & Vegetables		48
Glazed Carrots & Onions	70			
Green Bean Salad	100	Lazy Lasagne		18
Green Onion Sauce	38	Lemon Cheese Sauce		37
Green Pepper Sandwich	98	Lentil Soup		41
Grilled Corn on the Cob	110			
		Meatballs for Lovers		69
Ham, Cucumber & Cheese	96	Mediterranean Lamb Shanks & Vegetables		48
Heroine Sandwich	97			

Mexican Green Beans	57	Quick Clam Chowder	106
Minestrone Genovese	26		
Monday Night Meatball	7	Ranch House Beans	62
Montezuma Super Snack	65	Rice and ...	50
Muffled Carrot Muffins	34	Riviera Sandwich	95
		Roman Scampi	67
Nut loaf, The Health Nut's	24	Russian Eggplant	27
New Mexico Green Chile Chili	46	Russian Salad	101

Open Sesame Salad	83	Salads:	
Orange Toast with Honey Sauce	92	Avocado Stuffed with Salmon Salad	47
Parisian French Bread	82	Bean & Green Salad	30
Party Greenery	75	Bean Sprout Salad	68
Pasta:		Cannellini Bean Salad	100
Homemade Fettucine with Mushroom Sauce	9	Cottage Cheese Mix	58
Lazy Lasagne	18	Cucumber with Mint & Dill	100
Pasta & Bean Soup	11	Egg & Celery Salad	101
Son of Hamburger Helper	63	Green Bean Salad	101
Pasta & Bean Soup	11	Green Bean Salad	100
Peso-Pinchers	53	Open Sesame Salad	83
Piroshki	104	Party Greenery	75
Piquant Vegetable Sauce	38	Russian Salad	101
Plums in Port Sauce	76	Spinach & Lettuce Bowl	72
		Summer Fruit Salad	58
Quesadilla, Montezuma Super Snack	65	Tomato & Mozzarella Salad	83
		Tuna Salad	101
		Underground Potato Salad	112
		Zuper Zucchini	35

Velly Fast Chinese Chicken Salad	52
San Blas Surfer Steaks	109
Sandwiches:	
Apple, Cheese & Walnut	61
Avocado & Cheese	97
Bagel with Cream Cheese & Lox	96
Chicken & Cheese	61
Cottage Cheese & Avocado	61
Cream Cheese & Chicken	95
Cream Cheese Special	60
Danish Salmon Sandwich	60
El Hamburger	58
Green Pepper Sandwich	98
Ham, Cucumber & Cheese	96
Heroine Sandwich	97
Laguna Beach Hero	99
Riviera Sandwich	95
Salad Sandwich	61
Stuffed Ham Rolls	103
Tarzan & Jane's Raw Vegetable Surprise	23
The Late, Late Show	89
Tomato & Basil	98
Triple-Deck Salmon Sandwich	99
Tuna Fish & Cheese	96
Sangria, Cloud Nine	93
Salad Sandwich	61
Sauces:	
Green Onion Sauce	38
Guacamole Sauce	109
Lemon Cheese Sauce	37
Mushroom Sauce	10
Piquant Vegetable Sauce	38
Yogurt Sauce	37
Scrambled Eggs and . . .	57
Seafood:	
Avocado Stuffed with Salmon Salad	47
Danish Salmon Sandwich	60
Fresh Salmon Francaise	81
Roman Scampi	67
Tempura Without Tears	86
Triple-Deck Salmon Sandwich	99
Tuna Fish & Cheese Sandwich	96
Tuna Salad	101
Shanghai Chicken Stir-Fry	66
Six Friend Casserole	71
Son of Hamburger Helper	63
Soups:	
Chicken Soup That Mother Never Made	45
Gazpacho, Anyone?	105
Lentil Soup	41
Minestrone Genovese	26

Monday Night Meatball	7	The Friday Night Bird	54
Pasta & Bean Soup	11	The Second Time Around	15
Quick Clam Chowder	106	The Spinach Connection	62
The Ten-Minute French Onion Soup	56	Tomato & Basil	98
		Tomato & Mozzarella Salad	83
Won Ton From The Little Red Book	13	Triple-Deck Salmon Sandwich	99
		Tuna Fish & Cheese	96
Spiked Peaches	88	Tuna Salad	101
Spinach & Lettuce Bowl	72		
Spinach Gnocchi	25	Underground Potato Salad	112
Steak Satay	80		
Stuffed Baked Potato	57	Vegetables:	
Stuffed Ham Rolls	103	Baked Acorn Squash with Pineapple	36
Stuffed Eggs with Tuna Fish	102	Broccoli Spectacular	32
Summer Fruit Salad	58	Curried Green Beans	33
Sunday Thru Tuesday Pot Roast	20	Dr. Fu Manchu's Chinese Stir-Fry	29
Swiss Eggs	90	Glazed Carrots & Onions	70
		Grilled Corn on the Cob	110
Tacos, Day Before Payday Soy Grit	14	Mexican Green Beans	57
Tamale Pie	63	Russian Eggplant	27
Tarzan & Jane's Raw Vegetable Surprise	23	Spinach Gnocchi	25
Tempura Without Tears	86	Stuffed Baked Potato	57
The Best Beef Stew	43	Tarzan & Jane's Raw Vegetable Surprise	23
The Health Nut's Nut Loaf	24	The Spinach Connection	62
The Late, Late Show	89		
The Ten-Minute French Onion Soup	56		

Veiled Chicken	85
Velly Fast Chinese Chicken Salad	52
Won Ton From The Little Red Book	13
Yogurt Sauce	37
Zucchini Bread	51
Zuper Zucchini	35